I can't think of a more needed book for fathers, all types—blended families, foster fathers, non-custodial dads, adoptive fathers to wise elders and mentors. Dietrich Gruen effectively gets the reader to take a look at our biblical forefathers by pulling together these images and suggesting useful follow-up.

—Gary Smalley
President, Today's Family

Dietrich Gruen has written a thoughtful book, based on biblical father figures. Dietrich asserts, "When fathers get together and encourage one another, they can indeed make a difference." I agree. His book will be a great resource for your small group. Furthermore, this book is a winner, a long-term contribution for the father's movement, not just something faddish for the 90's.

—Ken Canfield
President, National Center for Fathering

Fathers Who Made a Difference *brings together many strands of Dietrich's life and ministry in small groups, in mentoring, and in fathering. His strength, as always, is asking insightful, interactive questions. This book represents a valuable Bible study resource that fathers of all types can use to strengthen their relationships.*

—E. Glenn Wagner
Vice President of National Ministries
Promise Keepers

FATHERS WHO MADE A DIFFERENCE

Dietrich Gruen

FATHERS WHO MADE A DIFFERENCE

Mistakes To Avoid And Models To Follow—15 Examples From The Bible

Nashville, Tennessee

Printed in the United States of America

ISBN 0-8054-1057-0

Product # 4210-57

Published by Broadman & Holman Publishers, Nashville, Tennessee

Some biblical forefathers and promise keepers profiled in this book have appeared elsewhere in print, in abbreviated or adapted form. Specifically, the profiles of Jephthah, Manoah, Eli, and David appeared in the *On the Father Front* newsletter (Christian Service Brigade: 1993-95); Elijah and Joseph in the *Today's Dads* newsletter (Wisconsin Fathers for Equal Justice: 1990-91).

Call-out quotes located at the beginning of every chapter are taken from Edythe Draper, *Draper's Book of Quotations for the Christian World* (Tyndale House Publishers, Wheaton, Illinois: 1992), unless otherwise noted.

Library of Congress Cataloging-in-Publication Data

Gruen, Dietrich, 1950–
Fathers who made a difference : mistakes to avoid and models to follow, 15 examples from the Bible / Dietrich Gruen.
p. cm.
ISBN 0-8054-1057-0
1. Fathers in the Bible. 2. Fatherhood—Religious aspects—Christianity. 3. Bible—Biography. I. Title.
BS579.F3G78 1995
220.8'3068742—dc20 94-42155
CIP

Dewey: 200.92
Sub.Hd: Fathers \ Bible—Biography

95 96 97 98 99 00 01 02 03 04 05 — 10 9 8 7 6 5 4 3 2 1

Table of Contents

"Do You Want a Fathering Course and Dad's Support Group?"

At recent Promise Keeper National Men's Conferences, and again at the 1994 Convention of the Christian Bookseller's Association, this author-father-promise keeper heard scores of urgent calls for fathers to rise up and take their rightful place in the home, church and community. I also read scads of newsletter, newspaper and magazine editorials in the last year—all targeting fathers.

From one conference alone, I came home with two suitcases full of materials on this topic! You might think I'd get pretty jaded from reading (or writing) yet another father's book.

Not so! I gladly join this growing chorus of voices calling for someone to speak to the "daddy stress" and "father hunger" now so evident in the workplace, home, and communities. Listen to a few of the voices that prompted me to joint the chorus and write this book:

On the social effects of absent fathers

> *Becoming husbands and fathers is the universal prescription of human societies for the socialization of the male. It is how societies link male aggression, energy, purpose—maleness—to a pro-social purpose. . . . The most important predictor of criminal behavior is not race, not income, not religious affiliation. It's father absence. It's boys who grow up without their fathers.*[1]
>
> —**David Blankenhorn,** Founder, Institute for American Values

On the need for training fathers in the church

> *We have weak churches because we have weak families; we have weak families because we have weak marriages; we have weak marriages because we have weak husbands and fathers; we have weak husbands and fathers because no one has ever trained them!*[2]
>
> —**Bill Gothard,** President, Basic Youth Conflicts

On man's innate desire to nurture children

Men who do not desire children will not have any and so their ignorance seals their fate. Men who look inside themselves will find something pulling them toward children—something pushing them to be a source of life. This force is alive and is strong within them. Some will recognize it for what it is, the call to be a father.[3]

—**E. James Wilder,** licensed clinical psychologist

On affirmative action programs for fathers

Men have to be persuaded that bringing up children is a very important part of their life. . . . My favorite affirmative action program would encourage men to associate with children: I would give men a mild preference to be kindergarten teachers, to be day-care workers. Motherhood has been praised to the skies, but the greatest praise men can give to that role is for them to share in doing it. That's my dream for the next generation.[4]

—**Ruth Bader Ginsburg,** Justice, U.S. Supreme Court

On reconnecting fathers and their children

Is it possible to reconnect fathers to their children? To reverse societal trends that produced the separation in the first place? To fashion government policies and reshape attitudes regarding fathers? To change the attitudes of fathers themselves? Probably. But not until we reconvince ourselves of what used to be common sense: Children need their fathers.[5]

—**William Raspberry,** syndicated columnist, *Washington Post*

[The Lord] will turn the hearts of fathers to their children and the hearts of children to their fathers.

—**Malachi** (4:6), God's messenger to Israel

How this book came to be

I invite you dads to reflect on how you were fathered and how you are fathering now. That's what I did to research and write *Fathers Who Made a Difference.* By maintaining this twin focus, the men in my Sunday School class at High Point Church helped to shape this book-in-process. From my parents I have received praise and support for my diligent efforts to parent as I was parented (if that worked) and to parent differently (where they may have made mistakes with me). This intergenerational learning continues in my present family. My wife and three sons have each tutored me in being a real dad; they have changed my life—not just this manuscript—for the better.

In drafting my character studies from Scripture, I must also credit inspiration from the *Serendipity Bible for Groups* and the *Word In Life Study Bible,* two long-term projects with which I was associated as contributing writer or editor. Thank you, Lyman, Dick, and Pete, for involving me and tutoring me in these Bible projects.

In writing this fathering book as a small group study guide, I benefited from all my editors and collaborators who mentored me in writing small group resources over the past two decades. You resource people know who you are. One in particular, Julia Pferdehirt, helped this manuscript take its final shape. I thank you one and all.

Who this book is for

I have listened to many fathers in the trenches, outside the church, who have something to say about this all-important task of fathering. They are the larger audience I have in mind for this book:

Ted has raised his son to be just like himself, an angry drunkard, and that scares him. He can only hope that his son will recover and be more successful at fathering than he was.

Jerry represents a number of emotionally and physically uninvolved fathers labeled "deadbeat dads." Fatherhood to him is more of a legal commitment defined punitively by the courts. His idea of fathering is based on what his ex-partner and the courts allow or enforce than on any inner model of his own.

Larry, an older man, no longer spends much time with his sons, not because of divorce, but because of changes in the work force. No longer are father and son involved in the family business. Without father-son intimacy on the job, many fathers don't know where to make up that lost time.

Another father I know, Stephen, took advantage of the work shifts made possible by the Information and Computer Age. He is now more physically present with his family as a stay-at-home dad. The challenge for him, and for other "Mr. Moms," is to develop the long-neglected nurturing aspect of his fathering.

Without kids of his own, Bill is a father in another sense. He fathers by "mentoring" through apprenticeship programs, tutoring in schools, and relating one-on-one with "disfathered" youths. He believes fatherhood is done best by a whole tribe of mature males, as in the African proverb: "It takes a whole village to raise a child."

Jay, a father in mid-life crisis, knew something was missing in his experience of fathering, but he was clueless. So he asked around. He then learned what he wanted and needed from his father and went about getting some of those needs met by meeting with other, older men who could give him what his dad couldn't.

The Teds, Jerrys, Larrys, Stephens, Bills, and Jays of this world, as well as those of church-based men's groups I know, give some flesh and blood to the men's groups I want to interact with in these chapters. I am dedicated to reaching them with the God of Abraham and Jacob. May their concerns, reflected in this book, stir up your consciousness of what being a father is all about, as they have mine.

TIPS FOR GETTING MORE OUT OF *FATHERS WHO MADE A DIFFERENCE*

The modern father's movement has emerged to affirm "father hunger" and heal male-woundedness. However, not seeing or feeling your father's love when you were small, or living with a remote and neglectful workaholic dad during your growing up years, is an injury not unique to boys. Girls experience the effects of *father hunger*, too.

For example, women who find it impossible to please an aloof, demanding father may spend their dating years doing anything and everything to get approval of a significant male. All daughters learn from their fathers what men are like and project that experience onto others ("all men are unfaithful," or "all men are abusive"). Cues taken from a father's reaction to his daughter help shape that woman's self-image for the rest of her life.

Hence, I invite you wives, mothers, and daughters to eavesdrop on the "mantalk" in this book. As you overhear men talk, laugh, and cry their way through the heady issues and heart-felt concerns presented in this interactive study guide, you will get some insight into the significant men in your life. If you adapt the mostly male illustrations and applications to your situation, you will also gain personal insight.

Nonetheless, this book *about* fathers is primarily *for* fathers. But it's not meant to be read alone, in a cave, as is the habit of some. Scout around your community, church, and workplace to find other fathers to interact with. Consider the needs not only of any children you still have at home, but also others for whom you could be a mentor, coach or father-figure. Ask the human resources folks at your office or the Christian education committee at your church to set up a fathering course or a dad's support group using this book.

The group leader is simply a *facilitator*, not a teacher or lecturer. All he needs is a willingness to share himself and listen to others. Facilitators don't need to have all the answers, just the questions. In fact, if you always have the answer, the group discussion will turn into a lecture.

Short thematic introductions profile the "dad of the week." Ask your group to read this ahead of time before coming together to tackle the follow-up questions. The group "warm-up" questions in each chapter help you to better get to know one another. Several questions for individual reflection or group study help you come to terms with a biblical dimension of fathering. A third set of questions are for application, to bring the point home to yourself and other fathers.

In sharing answers to this first and third set of questions, the group leader may want to review ground rules of confidentiality and model the level of trust and vulnerability he expects from others. Remember, the opening set of questions are designed with a low threshold of vulnerability, meant only to break the ice, warm up to each other with a chuckle, and introduce a theme related to the Bible study.

The third set of questions go much deeper—as deep as your example, group trust, and personal confidentiality will let you go.

As you read along with an open Bible, add your own words to mine. All three stirred together—your words, my words, and His Word, sprinkled with the words of others—that will help us fathers make a difference.

All that, and more, all here in one book. In the appendix, you'll find a short form of a father's survey administered by the National Center for Fathering (Shawnee, Kansas) under Ken Canfield. As Ken says, *One of the single most important tasks of a man's life is learning to father.* When you get to the end of this book profiling fathers from the Bible, you'll want help discovering and understanding your own father profile. Complete that survey and send it in to the National Center for Fathering. Then you will be given more opportunities for personal insight, seminar training, and small group resources for character formation and skill development in this all-important task of fathering.

I've written just enough to get you started; now it's your turn to open up and discover that when fathers get together and encourage one another, they can indeed make a difference. I pray the difference you make in your family and beyond will last for generations to come.

Endnotes

1. *Wisconsin State Journal,* April 25, 1993.
2. *Resource magazine,* May/June 1994.
3. E. James Wilder, *Life Passages for Men* (Servant Publications, Ann Arbor, MI: 1993), page 169.
4. *Wisconsin State Journal,* September 14, 1993.
5. *Wisconsin State Journal,* May 14, 1993.

—•••—

fa•ther *n* **1a:** a man who has begotten a child; *also* sire
Webster's Ninth (1983-)

—•••—

"Becoming a father is easy enough, but being one can be rough."
Wilhelm Busch (1832-1908)

—•••—

"Fathering is a marathon, not a sprint."
Paul L. Lewis (1944-)

—•••—

"O God, men think the heroes of tragedy great, and they admire them. But Abraham's contemporaries could not understand him. What then did he achieve? That he was true to his love. And he who loves God has no need of admiration, no need that others weep for him. He forgets his suffering in love, forgets it so thoroughly that no one even suspects his pain except thee, O God, who sees in secret, and knows the need, and counts the tears, forgetting nothing."
Soren Kierkegaard (1813-1855)

—•••—

CHAPTER ONE

Abraham and Other Wannabe Dads: Coping with the Pain of Childlessness

By Webster's first definition, we realize a man is not a father until he begets a child. But by experience and conviction, we know that having a child in the home makes one a real father no more than having a piano in the house makes one a musician.

Whereas *becoming a father* and *being a real dad* are two different enterprises, they are linked by a common decision, at least in planned families. In a planned family, this decision is made months, even years, before attempting (and succeeding) to conceive a child. In the case of the aging patriarch Abraham and his wife Sarah, it took 25 years of intentional effort and persevering faith to believe God for a child.

In modern times, with so many birth control and lifestyle options available, wannabe dads struggle all the more with this life-altering decision to have a child (or additional children). With modern birth control so ubiquitous (if not 100% effective!), more and more couples can and do wait until after their careers are established, or their checkbooks are balanced, before having a child. Other would-be dads and moms can't wait that long. Having made the decision to have a child in their "three-year post-college plan," they decide there and then to conceive. On the other hand, second-time around families, like mine, debate long and hard whether to have an "ours" baby after already having one of "hers" and two of "his."

Problems of Infertility

Nearly one in six couples are unable to conceive after delaying their decision and then commencing full-scale efforts to have a baby. Half of those couples will eventually succeed in having a baby of their own making or one of another's making.[1] (Whether we continuously plug away, undergo fertility testing and treatment, or pursue adoption, in any event, it is God who blesses with a "miracle baby.")

The other half of all childless couples must face the painful prospect of *never* having children of any kind. That means never having a child that bears your likeness. Childless couples never enjoy the obvious fruit of their love-making. Couples without any children miss the opportunity to leave their family mark and legacy to the world. Such losses cut deep wounds in the heart.

The childless couple also feels many outside pressures that complicate their situation. As her biological clock ticks away, others are there to remind her. Well-meaning family and friends are watching, hoping, and nosing around for a new addition. Inadvertently, couples with their children well in tow, can make the infertile couple feel awkward and envious.

Mourning the loss of something we never had is a very complex loss—one not warrantied at the hospital, nor covered by insurance, nor appreciated by couples blessed with children on their first try. Yet infertile couples must learn to grieve for the child they never had. Letting go of this dream, and the love they had stored up in anticipation of a baby, is crucial to a healthy resolution of infertility. Although society has become more accepting of the grief associated with miscarriage, still birth, or infant death, the experience of infertile couples is still a silent grief, largely misunderstood.[2]

When Men Lose Out on Having Children

If you want to be a father but can't, you will cope and grieve in a different way than will your wife. Because she carries the new life in her, undergoes the hormonal changes, senses the baby's fetal development and ever movement (even its hiccups), the once-pregnant woman suffers most acutely.

In the case of my wife's three miscarriages, she wanted each baby named and given an appropriate memorial service. When the due date for each baby came and went uneventfully, Sue was still grieving what once was and is no more. But she does not grieve alone.[3]

The loss for the expectant father is not as physiologically or as emotionally acute as it is for the grieving mother who has already bonded with their pre-born child developing in her uterus. While I did not experience the loss the same way as Sue did, this dad's loss was nonetheless real and painful. The lack of children is very unsettling and anger-producing for several reasons:

- *Would-be dads and moms struggle with their sexuality and self-image.* Church and society have defined gender roles, in large part, by the person's ability to father ("sire") or mother ("give birth to").
- *Would-be dads and moms fear loss of control.* Infertility treatment exposes their sex lives to medical experts and their high-risk, low-results procedures.

- *Would-be dads and moms suffer embarrassment* from nosy questions and "helpful" advice, as well as providing sexual history details and sperm specimens to doctors.
- *Would-be dads and moms hate pressure and insensitivity* from would-be grandparents, family members and friends. A friend's baby brings joy and hope mingled with deep pain to the infertile couple. Mother's Day at church can be unbearable.
- *Would-be dads and moms cry unfair!* when they see "undeserving" parents—especially neglectful and abusive parents, AFDC moms, or sexually active teens—having all the babies they don't want.
- *Would-be dads and moms try to win the blame game,* which pits husband against wife, in the hunt for who's at fault.
- *Would-be dads and moms succumb to guilt and shame,* as the infertile couple looks to their own hearts and to God for answers. ("What's wrong with me that I can't conceive? Is God punishing us for some reason, perhaps for an earlier abortion?")

The barren wife's double bind

In ancient patriarchal cultures, such as Israel's, infertility was a tragic bind for the woman. Bearing children was a sign of God's blessing, as in the case of Abraham, whom God promised would be a most blessed father of nations:

"I will make you into a great nation and I will bless you; I will make your name great, and you will be a blessing. . . . All peoples on earth will be blessed through you.... Count the stars—so shall your offspring be. . . . I will make nations of you and kings will come from you" (Genesis 12:2-3; 15:5; 17:6).

Just as children were received as an obvious blessing of God's provision, so childlessness was considered the dreaded curse of a "barren womb." In ancient Israel, infertility was considered so cursed shameful it was grounds for a man to divorce the woman and marry another who would bear him a child, preferably a son. (1 Samuel 1:3-8). (Makes you wonder if our biblical forefathers ever stopped to consider that infertility could, instead, have been the husband's problem.)

To keep their husband happy, some desperate women provided a surrogate mother to bear their hubby his most wanted child. That's what Sarah did for Abraham (Genesis 16:1-4) and Rachel did for Jacob (30:1-6). The manifold problems of sibling rivalries and blended families, stemming from multiple wives, are the subject of future chapters (see Chapter 2 on Jacob and Chapter 6 on David).

Abraham was 75 years old when God initially promised him offspring (Genesis 12:4); 86 years old when Ishmael was born to him by Hagar (16:16; 17:24-

25); and 100 years old when Isaac was born to him by Sarah (17:17; 21:1-3). Abraham's prolonged passage to fatherhood is instructive for us. He is commended to us as a model of faith, even "the father of all who believe" (15:6; Romans 4:11; Hebrews 11:7). Yet he was not unwavering in his faith, as we shall see.

Consider the irony in this synopsis: Abraham has no heir. He complains to God and puts forward a short-sighted, but culturally legitimate, compromise (15:1-3). His idea, to pass along his estate to his servant Eliezer is countered by God's promise (15:4-5). Abraham changes his mind and *agrees with God.* The childless Sarah likewise proposes an alternative, but culturally acceptable, means of producing a male heir. In her plan, Abraham impregnates Hagar, Sarah's maid-servant (16:1-2).[4] So Abraham changes his mind—again—to agree with Sarah, thus *disagreeing with God.* And this is the promise keeper hailed by Jews, Arabs, and Christians as "the father of all who believe?"

The lesson from Abraham's life for wannabe dads

The lesson from Abraham's life is both comforting and redemptive. Would-be fathers can cope with the pain of childlessness by drawing upon Abraham's exemplary faith. Despite prolonged childlessness, old age, and Sarah's barren womb, he believed God to make good His promise. As children of Abraham, we share in that faith, here and now.

Abraham was beset by various trials that could have undermined his call and his faith in God's promise to make him the "father of multitudes." Throughout these trials, Abraham maintained a deep, heart-felt faith in God. When this true "friend of God" (Isaiah 41:8; James 2:23) occasionally veered off the one sure passageway that God intended for him, God kept pulling him back from the brink.

That gives us hope that God will do as much for us who believe Him as He did for faithful Abraham. That does not mean that each cople will receive their longed-for, prayed-for child. Despite Abraham and Sarah's years of prayer and effort, their infertility lasted longer than a present-day lifetime.

Nor will heroic Abraham-like rescue efforts and Abraham-like intercessions guarantee that children in our custody respond favorably or turn out well.

Even Lot, Ishmael, and Isaac—all children under Abraham's charge—turned out differently, despite uniformly good parental intent. Lot's family did not all survive God's wrath on Sodom and Gomorrah, and even righteous Lot turned out to be a very sorry lot. Yet he would not have been saved at all without Abraham's persistent intercession. As for Ishmael and his descendants, they are presumed to be living under God's blessing (Genesis 17:18,20), but not without adversity (16:12).

Thus Abraham was a father who made a big difference in the lives of Lot, Ishmael, and Isaac—indeed, in the lives of all who truly believe. With Abraham-like faith, we fathers can also make a difference in our own families.

This biblical case study will focus not on the larger issues of justification by faith but, more narrowly, on what Abraham did to cope with childlessness. He remained faithful even though he was not initially fruitful.

Questions for Group Warm-up

These get-acquainted questions can be answered without reading the thematic introduction or doing the Bible study for this chapter.

1. To help you reflect on the blessings and challenges of your own family roots, and to appreciate the diversity within your group, answer the following questions. (Check as many boxes as apply.)

a. With whom did you spend your childhood?

- ☐ My natural parents
- ☐ Stepparents
- ☐ Blended family
- ☐ Orphanage
- ☐ Adoptive parents
- ☐ Single parent
- ☐ Other relatives
- ☐ Homeless shelter

b. As a child, who were the significant father figures in your life?

- ☐ Dear ol' Dad
- ☐ My favorite grandfather
- ☐ My Little League coach
- ☐ My tutor
- ☐ My youth group leader
- ☐ My stepdad
- ☐ My favorite uncle
- ☐ My high school coach
- ☐ My gang leader
- ☐ Other (please identify):

c. Who is the significant father-figure in your life now? (If your dad was never around, who was? If your dad has died, who, if anyone, has taken his place?)

2. For which kinds of "children" do you play a father-like role? Check and identify as many as apply. (This profile will be the basis for group sharing now and for application questions in the weeks to come.)

- ☐ Natural born children, ages and gender:
- ☐ Adopted children, ages and gender:
- ☐ Foster children, ages and gender:
- ☐ Grandchildren, ages and gender:
- ☐ Nephews and nieces, ages and gender:
- ☐ Homeless orphan, street kid, a fatherless child, or baby brother:
- ☐ Apprentices, players, or others you mentor, coach or "father":
- ☐ Other (please specify):

3. What three words describe your relationship with your extended family when you were a child? And now that you're an adult?

Questions for Bible Study

Read Genesis 12:1-5; 15:1-6; 16:1-6; 17:1-21; 21:1-7. Then continue your group study by individually answering these questions and sharing with others from your notes.

4. Abraham is one of those ancient promise-keepers "commended" for believing God (Hebrews 11:1-2) for "what we do not see?" (such as countless offspring and the enemy-held land of Canaan). However, his faith was not unwavering, but was full of trial and error. Some have counted up to ten trials of Abraham's faith and friendship with God, as recorded in Genesis 12-25. How many can you find in Genesis 15-17?

5. What must be going through their minds and hearts as Abraham and Sarah sincerely entertain these alternative ("Plan B") proposals that are clearly (to us) outside God's covenant ("Plan A")?

6. What problems or regrets, if any, did Abraham have with a passage to fatherhood (16:2-6)—a legitimate birth option in his day, but one which in our day looks like an adulterous affair and out-of-wedlock birth?

What problems or regrets did Sarah have with this messy (and fruitful!) solution to their parenting dilemma?

7. In what ways did God bless this alternative ("Plan B") proposal (16:10-16; also 17:20, fulfilled in 25:12-16)?

What problems or conflicts, typical of today's blended and second-time around families, do you think were created by the "late" arrival of Isaac, thirteen years after the birth of Ishmael (16:12)?

Questions for Application

This third set of questions is designed to bring the point home to yourself and other fathers.

8. "By faith Abraham...was enabled to become a father" (Hebrews 11:11). How has your own waiting period or eventual passage to fatherhood affected your faith in the God of promise? (And vice versa: how has your faith enabled your parenting?)

- ☐ Seeing the miracle of life made a believer out of me.
- ☐ I, too, have laughed and cried at the prospect of fathering a child well beyond the normal child-bearing or child-rearing years.
- ☐ Having a child increased my faith and prayer.
- ☐ I gave up doing things my way and began trusting God to do what He wants in and through me and my child.
- ☐ I have surrendered my offspring to God, to use their lives for His total approval and purpose.
- ☐ My days have been dark and insufferable as midnight blackness, but then I could see the stars and was reminded of God's sure promise to Abraham.
- ☐ In His mysterious way, the life God gives He takes away, as He did with my failed pregnancy, or with my child taken in the prime of youth.
- ☐ My children impress on me the need for more Christian education, both for them and for myself.
- ☐ It may be too late to become a father, but it's never too late to be a real dad.
- ☐ Other (please explain):

9. What aspect of your parenting are you now depending on God to fulfill in His own way—perhaps in a way that is "laughable" and "fruitful," even beyond what you could ask or think?

10. Perhaps you, or some in your study group, have failed to get pregnant over a long period of time. Maybe some others have repeatedly suffered failed pregnancies or false hopes of adoption. Ask around. With the help and empathy of a friend like Abraham, listen to one another share about what it's like "when men lose out on having children" (review pages 8-9). Then pray about them in your group, or in pairs, as you have time.

11. **(Optional)** The rest of Abraham's story (see below) makes the point that *you can be a real dad without or before becoming a biological father.* Apply the suggested possibilities to your own situation, especially if you are childless. How could you be a *real dad* without having children of your own?

THE REST OF THE STORY

The childless Abraham had family and fathering responsibilities and opportunities to be a real dad *long before Ishmael or Isaac came along.* After his father's death in Haran (in modern-day Iraq), Abraham became the patriarch of a large, extended family. When he set forth for Canaan (Genesis 12:1), only a few family members accompanied him. Among the family he took with him was his bright, entrepreneurial nephew Lot. Lot was always getting into trouble—from which Abraham had to rescue him (Genesis 13-14; 18-19).

Older singles and childless men can be fathers in various ways by following the example of Abraham. You can be a father figure to the extended family members younger than you. Opportunities abound with any nieces, nephews, or younger cousins who live nearby—especially, but not exclusively, those without a father regularly in the home. Thus Uncle Abraham was a father to Lot, cousin Mordecai was a father to Esther.

Many social organizations exist to help you find the child outside your extended family with whom you can share your life as a supplemental or surrogate father: Big Brother/Big Sister programs, the Scouts, Little League baseball, Sunday school, confirmation class, youth groups, community clubs, or camp counselor. Once children reach an age when they are actively exploring their world, this provides all men an opportunity to be a coach or mentor, sharing their wisdom, vision, or interest in sports, the arts or some hobby.

Once you find your little guy or little girl to nurture along the way to adulthood, you'll find yourself asking, "Now, what would a father do in this situation?" In the spiritual sense of fathering we ask, "What would an Elijah, or father-like tutor do for an apprentice like Elisha?" Or "What would an elder like Paul do for a young protégé like Timothy?" Or, more to the point of this study, we ask "What would father Abraham do in this situation if this were his nephew Lot?"

The fruitful, happy ending to Abraham's and Sarah's story is Isaac, but that is ***not*** the norm for all childless couples. We can't say that giving birth to a child after years of futility is the only happy ending for a man or woman of faith. God sometimes chooses for a particular couple not to have children. Jesus calls some to be "eunuchs for the kingdom." This calling can apply to childless men who regard their limitation as a vocation, as well as to those men who renounce marriage for a higher calling (Matthew 19:12; 1 Corinthians 7:7-8).

Situations like singleness or childlessness, which are often not our choice can become godly callings when we come to see and accept the inherent possibilities and opportunities. To be child*less* is thus to be child*free,* just as to be without a spouse is to be free of worldly concern (1 Corinthians 7:32-35); in both cases God can use us in ways not possible if we were encumbered with family responsibilities.

By reflecting on such questions, we begin acting like a real father in the life of that child—blessing them with the love of God and praying for them with the persistence of Abraham. With Abraham-like faith, we fathers can also make a difference in building up our families. . .even if God should not grant us children of our own.

Our Next "Dad of the Week"

The story of Abraham and his sons is not the only example of a troubled, expectant dad highlighted in the Bible. The continuing saga of Abraham brings us, two generations later, to Jacob and his twelve sons. Together, they illustrate the bane and blessing of blended families.

The story of Jacob and his extended family covers twenty-five chapters in Genesis, providing enough material for two case studies of Jacob. In preparation for the first Jacob profile, which traces his pursuit of the blessing, read Genesis 27:1-40; 29:31-30:24 with 35:16-19; also 32:22-30. In preparation for the second Jacob profile which traces family favoritism, read Genesis 37 and 48-49. As you read this extended biblical narrative, reflect on what it means to be a "Partisan Patriarch."[5]

Endnotes

1. Sue Vander Hook and Rachel Kiepe, *Infertility* (Serendipity House, Littleton, CO: 1991).

2. Persons with problems of infertility are encouraged to contact RESOLVE, Inc. at 1310 Broadway, Somerville, MA 02144, or call the helpline 617/623-0744. Founded in 1973, this 25,000-member organization works with infertile couples and associated professionals, such as adoption workers, doctors and counselors. RESOLVE, Inc., offers a national newsletter, information & referrals, and peer-support groups at the local level.

3. Individuals who have experienced miscarriages, ectopic pregnancies, still births or a newborn's death are encouraged to contact RTS Bereavement Services at 1910 South Ave, La Crosse, WI 54601, or call the helpline 1-800/362-9567, ext. 4747. Founded in 1981 as Resolve Through Sharing, this perinatal bereavement program is based in over 1000 hospitals in the United States and abroad. Local hospital groups offer bereavement counseling, courses in health care, professional materials and support services for family members.

4. Note that, in ancient Near Eastern culture, a childless man could legitimately adopt a favorite male servant to become his heir apparent and custodian of his estate. Ancient custom at the time of the patriarchs, as illustrated in the historic Code of Hammurabi (1792-1750 B.C.), also permitted the practice of sleeping with a maid servant to ensure the birth of a male heir.

5. If you and your group have time in your schedule for only 13 weekly discussions, you may decide to either: (a) combine Parts I and II of the Jacob narrative (Chapter 2); or else, (b) skip one or the other half of Chapter 2. (The same options apply to the two-part Chapter 6.)

—•••—

"You can choose to be a bag of marbles . . . independent, hard, loud, unmarked, and unaffected by others. Or you can be a bag of grapes . . . fragrant, soft, blending, mingling, flowing into one another's lives. Marbles are made to be counted and kept. Grapes are made to be bruised and used. Marbles scar and clank. Grapes yield and cling."

Charles R. Swindoll (1934-)

—•••—

"One wrong assumption—that blended families are like original nuclear families with just a few more people here and there—can be hazardous to your mental health. Blended families have a more complex structure and extra problems which seem to descend from nowhere.

Tom & Adrienne Frydenger, *The Blended Family*

—•••—

CHAPTER TWO, PART I

Jacob and Other Partisan Patriarchs: Blending Multiple Parent Families and Scheming for "The Blessing"

Today's patchwork family is not all that blended or blissful. I have yet to meet a happily blended family like "The Brady Bunch" of TV fame. Nor do I know any perfectly loving, all-everything stepmothers like Julie Andrews in *The Sound of Music.* In fact, many second-time-around families today are hurting, some even hateful. On a bad day, modern stepmoms seem as wicked as Cinderella's. Likewise, some stepdads seem equally evil—carrying grudges against their ex-wives, abusing their new families, not stopping until they land in jail or the grave.

All the above are stereotypes, to be sure. I propose a more useful one: Some multi-parent/multi-kid families are like "The Jacob Dozen" of ancient Israel. To appreciate the relevance of Jacob as the patriarch of today's blended family, we need to draw out a few of the connections.

The Jacob Dozen

Note, first of all, that The Jacob Dozen was a "baker's dozen" consisting of twelve sons and one daughter (Dinah). They have four moms but the same dad. In your mind's eye, suppose this complex blended family was featured on a prime-time TV sitcom. Hollywood would recast and update the family's central father figure, rendering him as four more of *today's dads.* Cast in the father role might be the emotionally distant "absentee father," the financially well-off but "deadbeat dad," and the unwed or undetermined "paternity case." Toss in a floating "uncle" or two and a host of "significant others," and the cast of today's dads is complete and politically correct. Rather than attribute all thirteen children to one "patriarch" (a throwback term from a bygone, father-knows-best era), our modern TV version casts doubt on the paternity of every child in The Jacob Dozen by introducing a more complete cast of father figures.

All such ingredients might bring good ratings, but in a real life family, they make for poor blending.

"My Four Moms" produce The Jacob Dozen

A contemporary remake of leading women in The Jacob Dozen calls for a few changes: one "wicked stepmother" or "wicked ex-" (Leah), one surrogate mom (Bilhah), a "femme fatale" or sweet mistress (Zilpah), the traditional "lady of the house" (Rachel), and a damsel in distress (daughter Dinah). Rachel would have the best lines, of course, as she plays the forlorn and suicidal woman, taunted by three Fertile Myrtles. In the end, Rachel gets what she wants—another child. That Rachel dies in childbirth (Genesis 35:16-19) is ironic in light of her wish: "Give me children, or I'll die" (30:1).

To strengthen the contemporary link for the many second-time-around fathers in our viewing audience, we would also have to revise Jacob's marital history. Jacob's complex marital arrangement would shock even jaded prime-time viewers. Who of us engages in *polygamy* (marriage in which either husband or wife may legally have more than one mate), or *polygyny* (where this more-than-one-mate privilege was limited to the husband), or *bigamy* (entering into marriage with one person while still legally married to another)? After all, monogamy was God's original intention (Genesis 2:23-24). Yet polygamy and polygyny were practiced by godly men like Jacob in ancient times.

Today's serial marriages: polygyny in another form

As painful as divorce is to our moral sensitivities, it is not outlawed today, although our country has legally prohibited polygamy, polygyny, and bigamy. Hence, to fit Jacob's blended family into these politically correct times, a few ex-wives would complete the family tree and compete for Jacob's attention. Each new wife/concubine Jacob takes on would require him to divorce the previous one. In which case, he would have married and divorced Leah once, leaving him with child support obligations for four sons. Later on, when Jacob would produce three more legitimate children by Leah, he'd have to remarry her. But to have his final two sons by Rachel, he'd then have to divorce Leah a second time.

That scenario may sound fanciful, as it does not square with the Jacob we know. But suppose Jacob lived in our century, under Westernized marital laws, where polygyny is outlawed and child support court-ordered. He would owe child support for almost a dozen children stemming from four women he had to marry and unmarry, each in turn! Can you sympathize with Jacob picking up the tab for this circus-like serial marriage? The guy who said, "They're cheaper by the dozen!" didn't know The Jacob Dozen.

Purists will complain that such modern revisionism is taking too much liberty with the original script. I agree. However, such a stretched script does line up with current anthropological and sociological research. Robert Wright, a senior editor at *New Republic*, claims, "Around 1000 of the 1154 past or present societies studied by anthropologists have permitted a man to have more than one wife. Today's serial marriages, so common among the well off, can be seen as polygyny in another form."[1]

The Jacob-like sitcom, which I dubbed "My Four Moms," reflects this research. But such a TV remake of Jacob's family departs from the original script found in Genesis 29:31-30:24. For more about this complex blended family, as it was and as it applies to you, stay tuned to the study section which follows this narrative portion.

Matt's Four Moms and The Gruen Group

Along with this "My Four Moms" theme, I invite you to observe our reconstituted family: the not-yet-ready-for-prime-time "Gruen Group." If you had been a sociologist observing us anytime during the first four years we were still blending, you would have noticed that Matt also has "four moms." He regularly spends time with four women who have all helped rear him: his birth mother (Sue); his stepmom (Lynne); his maternal grandma (Rosemary); and his paternal great grandmother ("G.G."). Matt is the richer—socially, spiritually and materially—for having multiple parents. (Whenever he gets bored or exhausts one household, he just goes to another one.) Such is the *blessing* of blended families.

What about the *bane* of blended families? Raised by different sets of parents, Christian and non-Christian, also introduces conflicting sets of family values. Children with multiple parents get multiple messages and thus don't know what's expected of them. Our family is no exception.

When Matt and my two boys are at this house (an every-other-week occurrence), you might observe the following troublesome dynamics. Suppose you found my sons and stepson all in the same room doing or saying the same obnoxious things (not an unlikely scenario). You then see my stepson Matt get on my nerves, while my sons Eric and Mark do not. Likewise for my wife. Eric and Mark get on Sue's nerves, whereas she's usually oblivious to her own son's insults or obnoxious behavior.

Jacob was no exception to this rule. He, too, experienced the bane and the blessing of blending his hybrid family.

Jacob's Continuing Search for The Blessing

God's blessing of Jacob and his family helps fulfill His promise to Abraham, which was to give him nations from his offspring. The fruitfulness of siring twelve sons who become the twelve tribes of Israel fulfills this promised blessing. Yet Jacob continues to search for something more. His hunger and struggle for the blessing is what endears this patriarch of blended families to those us who wrestle with the same fathering issues.

By deception, Jacob wrested away the blessing from his earthly father (Isaac).

Then Jacob fell into desperate straits at the hands of both his treacherous uncle (Laban) and his estranged and vengeful brother (Esau). A fearful, guilt-ridden, on-the-run Jacob tried to escape his past (Genesis 27-32). But the sins of our past do have a way of catching up with us, and trading in wives or having more kids never satisfies what is basically a spiritual hunger.

Hence, Jacob eventually had to contend all night with God's angel until he wrestled away another blessing, this one from his heavenly Father (Genesis 32:22-30). In the language of the modern psychology and the recovery movement, we might say that Jacob was experiencing and expressing genuine "father hunger."

Everyone hungers for blessing. When fathers fail to bless, children grow up with deep, unconsciously expressed father hunger. Some people desperately seek in new mates what they are lacking in a vital relationship with their own fathers. In women, this father hunger manifests itself in searching promiscuously and vainly for a man to give the kind of time and attention and acceptance that only a father can give.

This father hunger also has a relational and spiritual dimension for men. Father hunger may have driven Jacob to reconcile with Esau (32:1-21; 33:1-15) and with God (32:22-30). There was a God-shaped vacuum in Jacob's life, in spite of the fact—no, *because* of the fact—he had already schemed to get the coveted blessing from Isaac and Esau.

The study questions which follow will explore both aspects of blended families: the bane and the blessing. Let us consider how this partisan patriarch managed his extended family, one richly blessed by God.

Questions for Group Warm-up

These get-acquainted questions can be answered without reading the thematic introduction or doing the Bible study for this chapter.

1. About your family of origin, how many siblings did you grow up with?

   b. How many parent figures (aunts, uncles, stepparents, grandparents) did you grow up with?

2. Where were you in the birth order of your original family? (How did that change, if and when your family suddenly blended with another?)

   - ☐ I was an only child (a perfectionist, spoiled rotten).
   - ☐ I was the firstborn (who felt the need to control others).
   - ☐ I was a middle child (who always felt squeezed out).
   - ☐ I was the baby of the family (who "got away with murder").
   - ☐ Other (please explain):

Questions for Bible Study

Read Genesis 29:31-30:24; 35:16-19 with 49:1-28; 32:22-30. Then continue your group study by individually answering these questions and sharing with others from your notes.

3. The twelve sons of Jacob, raised in adversity, became the twelve tribes of Israel, blessed for posterity. Look at both the NIV textual footnotes, which define their Hebrew birth names (Genesis 29:31-30:24; 35:16-19), and the word pictures which Jacob used to illustrate their respective destinies (49:1-28). What is significant about these twelve named sons? *(Different group members can research one or more apiece and report their findings to the group.)*

- ☐ Reuben (29:32; 49:3-4):
- ☐ Simeon (29:33; 49:5-7):
- ☐ Levi (29:34; 49:5-7):
- ☐ Judah (29:35; 49:8-12):
- ☐ Dan (30:6; 49:16-17):
- ☐ Naphtali (30:8; 49:21):
- ☐ Gad (30:11; 49:19):
- ☐ Asher (30:13; 49:20):
- ☐ Issachar (30:18; 49:14-15):
- ☐ Zebulun (30:20; 49:13):
- ☐ Dinah (30:21):
- ☐ Joseph (30:24; 49:22-26):
- ☐ Benjamin (35:18; 49:27):

4. We have drawn two configurations of Jacob's complex family on pages 22-23. Figure 1 represents a genogram of Jacob's family tree, as some genealogist might draw it. Figure 2 represents a sociogram of Jacob's family table as some family therapist might draw it. Suppose you were a family therapy consultant asked to review the "Jacobson file" in light of these two diagrams: What might this file on the Jacobsons tell you about the bane and blessing of a patriarchal blended family?

Figure 1

GENOGRAM OF JACOB'S FAMILY TREE

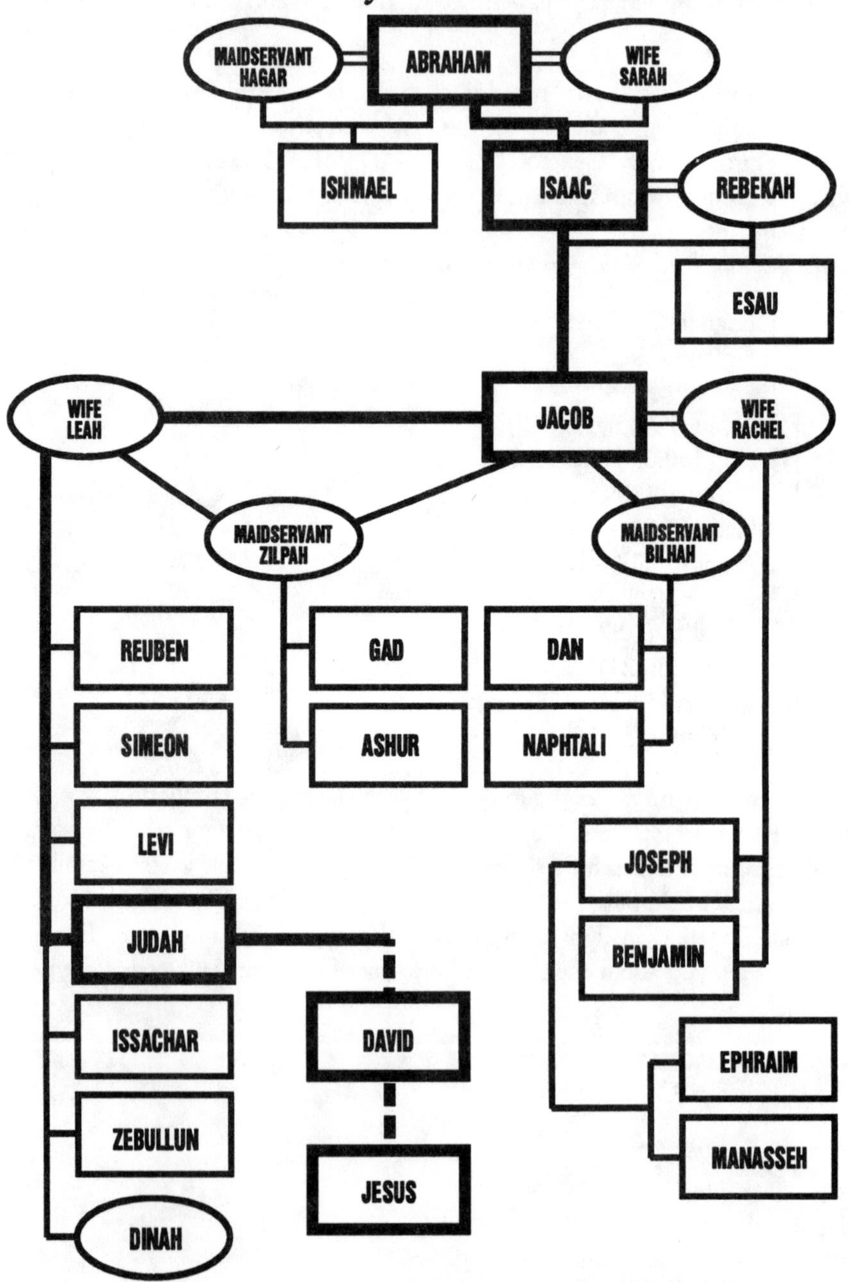

Figure 2

SOCIOGRAM OF JACOB'S FAMILY TREE

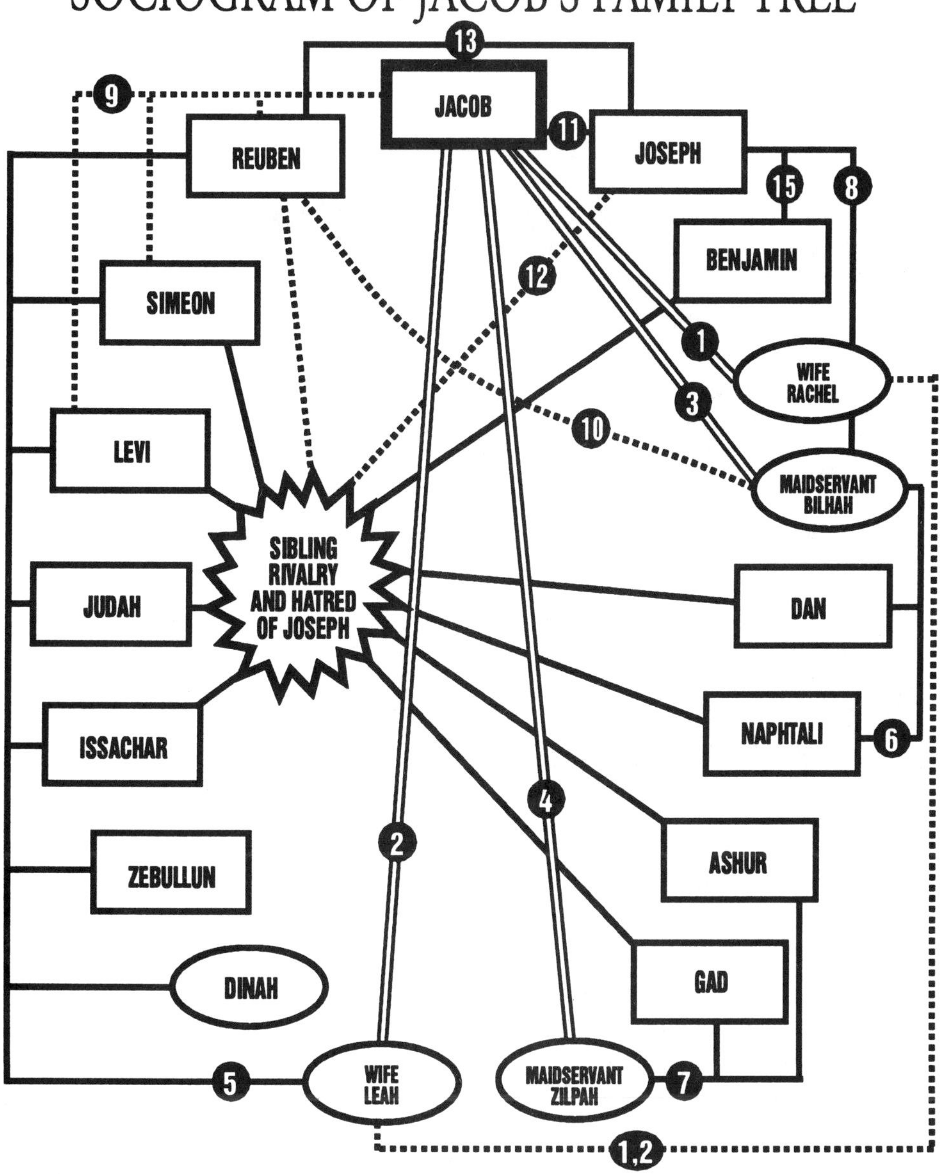

1,2 Genesis 29:16-30
3 Genesis 30:3-4
4 Genesis 30:9
5 Genesis 29:31-35, 30:17-21
6 Genesis 30:5-8
7 Genesis 30:9-13
8 Genesis 30:22-24, 35:16-19
9 Genesis 34:30, 49:5-7
10 Genesis 35:22, 49:4
11 Genesis 37:3, 31-35, 46:14, 48:1-22
12 Genesis 37:4-28, 45:4-5, 50:15-21
13 Genesis 37:21-22, 29, 42:22
14 Genesis 42:38, 44:20, 30
15 Genesis 43:29-34, 45:14

5. Jacob could not prosper without the blessing of God (Genesis 32:22-30). What do you find most promising about Jacob hungering for, and ultimately finding, not only the blessing of his earthly father, but also of his heavenly Father?

- ☐ Jacob could not run from his past without God's blessing; nor can we.
- ☐ Jacob could not manage his complex blended family without some outside help from God; neither can we.
- ☐ Jacob could not find satisfaction in the accumulation of wealth or possessions; neither can we.
- ☐ Jacob realized his need for spiritual strength and divine favor, which eluded him in all his other relationships and schemes.
- ☐ Not even his many wives and sons could compensate for an aching void within, one only God could fill.
- ☐ Jacob confronts the myth of the self-made man, which still has its grips on so many today.
- ☐ Other (please explain):

Questions for Application

This third set of questions is designed to bring the point home to yourself and other fathers.

6. The sitcom "My Four Moms" and the spinoff series "The Jacob Dozen" both have some hilarious possibilities, depending on who is cast for what roles. You'll find the original script for this TV remake in Genesis 29:31—30:24. There you'll see the bane and blessing of blended families. Perhaps you'll recognize the families you came from, the families you married into, or the family you have now. In that regard, which of the following from Jacob's family do you see in your own family history:

- ☐ A spurned, unloved first wife (29:31,33).
- ☐ Vain attempts to win the husband's attention (29:34).
- ☐ Jealousy of a rival sister sleeping with her husband (30:1).
- ☐ A threatened suicide ["Give me children, or I'll die!"] (30:1).
- ☐ Anger and blame-shifting by a trapped husband (30:2).
- ☐ Years of infertility, long waits for a child, then a "surprise" (30:22-24).
- ☐ The life and death choice between a pregnant mother's health and her unborn child (35:16-19).

7. Jacob hungered to know the blessing in four vital relationships: (a) his father, (b) his brother, (c) his employer, and (d) his God. At what points can you identify with Jacob's hunger for divine favor?

a. *As conferred by Isaac, his aging father* (Genesis 27:18-29; 31:53): Do you sense your father's blessing in any material, relational or spiritual way? Why?

b. *In reconciling with Esau, the estranged brother Jacob betrayed* (25:31-34,35,41; 32:3-21; 33:1-15): Do you have any family relationships that need reconciling? How might you go about that?

c. *In reconciling with Uncle Laban, his father-in-law and former employer* (30:25-31:3,31,43-44,53): Do you have estranged relationships at work that need reconciliation? What step can you take, following Jacob, to make things right?

d. *For his heavenly Father, who blessed him with many children, material wealth, a new name, the divine presence, and a special future* (27:28-29; 28:3-4,16,20-21; 31:3; 32:1,9-12,24- 30): Do you sense God's blessing? Or are you still wrestling with Him over some unfilled desire?

The Rest of the Story

Read Genesis 25-33 to see how "the rest of the story" plays out in Jacob's search for a blessing that only a father can give. Yes, Jacob is one of those fathers who, by being blessed, could make a real difference in his family. In the continuation of Jacob's story (Chapter 2, Part II), we see how he was able to pass on the blessing he finally received. Jacob blesses his twelve sons, but does so in a very partisan way, playing favorites with Joseph and Joseph's two sons, Manasseh and Ephraim.

Our Next "Dad of the Week"

In preparation for this next installment of the Jacob story, read Genesis 37 and 48:1—49:28. You might want to skim the chapters in between. As we take a second look at what it means to be a "Partisan Patriarch," we will reflect on the bane and the blessing of playing favorites in blended families.

Endnotes

1. Quoted in *Time*, August 15, 1994, and adapted from Robert Wright's book, *The Moral Animal: Evolutionary Psychology and Everyday Life* (Pantheon, 1994).

—•••—

"Man is probably the only animal which ever attempts to have anything to do with his half-grown children."
George Ross Wells (1884-1962)

—•••—

"Alas! if my Friend, who laid down his life for me, were to remember all the instances in which I have neglected him, and to plead them against me in judgment, where should I hide my guilty head in the day of recompense? I will pray, therefore, for blessings on my friends, even though they cease to be so, and upon my enemies, though they continue such."
William Cowper (1731- 1800)

—•••—

CHAPTER TWO, PART II

Jacob, Joseph and Other Partisan Patriarchs: The Bane and Blessing of Playing Favorites in Blended Families

Stepbrothers often feel like ruling over and seeking revenge toward one another for real or perceived hurts, as occurred in Jacob's family. One reason for this tendency toward violence is that stepparents do not naturally feel the same way about all "his" and "her" children. For years this was a source of shame and guilt for me, as I am a very nurturing-type guy. I pledged at my wedding to love and discipline Matt as if he were my own son. Later, after failing to keep this wedding vow, I came to wonder, "How can I call myself a Christian and have hateful feelings toward this kid?"

To overcome this estrangement and strengthen our blended family, I had to learn that love is *not* primarily some feeling we conjure up, but an unconditional concern or commitment for the other's total well-being. Overcoming the reticence to talk about, and own up to negative feelings, has strengthened our stepfamily. My openness and vulnerability in this regard has given others permission to be more honest too. (When I first married, I thought a Christian exercising faith should not, or could not, experience negative feelings. *Either I am not a true believer or else, if I am, then I must not be feeling anything negative.* Or so I thought.)

In stepfamilies, the parents must learn to share honest feelings but to "co-conduct" their family rules and discipline. In a nuclear family, Mom and Dad have twelve or more years, let's say, to work out and blend their individual parenting styles *before* some adolescent exposes their inconsistencies. With enough time for (step)parent-child bonding during the grade school years, those challenging teenage years are more manageable.

However, in a nontraditional, multi-parent mix of half-brothers and "someone else's kids"—such as Jacob's family and mine—those parenting styles are pre-established, hard to merge, and bound to conflict. Can you imagine yourself as one of those twelve sons with five semi-related parents, each with a different idea how you should behave yourself? (It's bad enough with three; how does one manage with twelve?)

Take that a step further: Imagine yourself as a parent with no previous history with someone else's teenager. Some "know-it-all" and "I-don't-know-you" teenage stepson is suddenly in your face, bringing out the worst in you. (I've heard it said, "Adolescence is that period in a child's life when his parents become more difficult to manage.") That's what often happened to Matt and me when I first became his unwanted, unfamiliar stepfather. Lest I ever forget my mistakes with Matt, Sue (who can be equally partisan, favoring her son over mine) is there to remind me.

Partisan Patriarchs: Like Father, Like Son

Gary Smalley, renown author and speaker for Focus on the Family, Promise Keepers, and for his own organization, Today's Family, has written many books about the family blessing. Smalley draws upon the Genesis account of Jacob's "last will and testament" to define The Blessing in terms of its five essential elements:[1]

* *Meaningful Touch*
* *A Spoken Message*
* *Attaching "High Value" to the One Being Blessed*
* *Picturing a Special Future for the One Being Blessed*
* *An Active Commitment to Fulfill the Blessing*

While this family blessing is a good thing, too much of a good thing can create problems. Partisan parenting and the pretentious pursuit of "The Blessing" is what got Jacob and his favorite son Joseph into big-time trouble with the other offspring (Genesis 37).

Partisan parenting will land families in trouble most every time—especially when the favorite son (child #11, Rachel's firstborn) always gets to be king of the hill. Jacob played favorites with Joseph, a living example of the proverbial truth, "Children learn what they live."

If a child lives with favoritism, he learns to play favorites. Jacob played and plotted for his father Isaac's favor or blessing, always outwitting and infuriating his brother Esau (Genesis 25:23-34; 27:1-41). Should it surprise us if Jacob now behaves as a father the way he did as a child?

No. Instead, we find fault with Joseph. A product of his father's partisan parenting, Joseph became so full of self-importance that he brazenly provokes his brothers to bear-like anger and revenge. Shortly after his dreams of self-importance, the "lowly" brothers gang up to ambush Jacob's favorite son, consigning him to life in the pits—first in a deep water well and later in the slave economy of Midianite traders.

No doubt the patriarch's favor toward Joseph now felt more like a curse. If Jacob had treated everyone equally, the other eleven brothers would have had no reason to gang up on Joseph. While Joseph could have shifted blame onto his father for this pitfall, he did not. Perhaps he reasoned that Jacob didn't know any better than to parent the way he had been parented. Even his grandfather Abraham was a partisan patriarch, preferring the younger Isaac over the older Ishmael which, in turn, led to centuries of predictable conflict between their descendants (Genesis 16:12).

Talk about intergenerational, dysfunctional families! Today's psychology textbook on "dysfunctional blended families" (that's a redundancy in terms) must have taken a page from this Genesis account ofThe Jacob Dozen. One current Broadway musical takes its entire script from this powerful chapter. (Have you seen "Joseph and the Amazing Technicolor Dream Coat?" Please do.) Such is the *bane* of blended families.

The Blessing of Blended Families

Partisan parenting is not always all bad, as it turns out. Jacob's blessing of the two grandsons by Joseph (Genesis 48:18-20) and then of all twelve sons (49:1-28), makes for a fascinating study with contemporary application to good fathering. In his own partisan but appropriate way, a dying Jacob blesses each and every member of his extended family.

At the end of his life, Jacob blessed Ephraim ahead of Manasseh (48:18-20). Jacob once more demonstrated the truth that children learn what they live. Jacob was the younger son of Isaac, yet secured the firstborn's blessing; he also preferred the younger sister Rachel to the older Leah. So also Manasseh was the younger of Joseph's two sons, but Jacob gave him the firstborn's coveted blessing.

Such is the way of a partisan patriarch and a sovereign God.

In this respect, Jacob's partisan parenting lines up with current dogma for stepparents: Do not strive to love and motivate each child *equally*, but rather care for each one *uniquely*, according to their particular needs, natural bent, and "the best interests of the child." Divorce courts have their own slippery definition for that legal, catch-all phrase ("best interests"), but so does Jacob, who pictures a special, but different future for each of twelve sons.

The study questions to follow will focus more on what this partisan patriarch did to bless his extended family.

Questions for Group Warm-up

These get-acquainted questions can be answered without reading the thematic introduction or doing the Bible study for this chapter.

1. What do you think is the ideal size for a "functional family" and why?

2. Which relationship, in either your family of origin or your present family, generates the most conflict or stress?

- ☐ Father-son
- ☐ Father-daughter
- ☐ Brother-brother
- ☐ Sister-sister
- ☐ Ex-spouses
- ☐ Mother-son
- ☐ Mother-daughter
- ☐ Brother-sister
- ☐ Parents and their stepchildren
- ☐ Other (please explain):

Questions for Bible Study

Read Genesis 37:2-36; 48:1—49:28. Then continue your group study by individually answering these questions and sharing with others from your notes.

3. The sibling rivalry between Joseph and his brothers is legendary—full of pathos, intrigue and irony. The apparent death of the beloved-yet-hated Joseph hurt the partisan patriarch terribly (Genesis 37).

a. Why do you suppose Jacob took it so hard?

b. Were the brothers prepared for that strong reaction? Why or why not?

c. Was this a crime of *opportunity*, one of *passion*, or was it *premeditated*? Why do you think so?

4. What elements of the five-fold blessing do you see in Jacob's "last will and testament" concerning two of his grandsons, the children of Joseph (Genesis 48:1-20)?

b. What was unusual about the way Jacob blessed Ephraim and Manasseh, contrary to Joseph's expectations? Why did he do that?

5. Reread question 3 in Part I of Jacob's story (page 21). Reflect on what it must have been like for each son to seek the blessing, and then to receive the particular blessing he gave. With which of the twelve can you closely identify?

Questions for Application

This third set of questions is designed to bring the point home to yourself and other fathers.

6. When Joseph was seventeen, his brothers hated him, with good reason. The resulting decisions, meant for evil, God used for good to shape "the Jacobsons" and the future of Israel for generations to come. Use the space below to diagram your own family interactions when you were a teenager. Picture a gathering of your family clan,

positioning everyone in their usual seats at the dinner table. Use boxes and circles to designate males and females. Connect them with lines of communication around the table to indicate the kind or quality of relationships. Add any explanatory footnotes or captions you wish.[2] You may wish to include branches tying in extended family members, such as: grandparents and grandchildren; any ex-spouses and their mates; all stepchildren and foster kids; any aunts, uncles and cousins you see during the year. Don't forget "significant others."

7. In Genesis 48, we see two of Jacob's grandsons competing for the coveted blessing of the man they most admired. Manasseh is passed over. Likewise in Genesis 49, some of Jacob's sons received more curse or rejection than blessing for their sinful past. Jacob's daughter received no mention at all. Put yourself in their place.

a. How would you have felt if you were the slighted Manasseh?

b. . . . the cursed Reuben, Simeon, or Levi?

c. . . . the neglected Dinah?

d. Did you ever try to manipulate your parents or grandparents into giving you special attention or preferential treatment? How so?

8. Now put the shoe on yet another foot. Imagine yourself as Ephraim, on the receiving end of a substantial blessing from an esteemed father figure. If you were in a position of being deeply loved by the man you most admire, as was Ephraim, what feelings would that create in you, and what actions might that prompt you to take?

9. In Genesis 49, we see Jacob's twelve sons vying for the final portion of that blessing. Some evidently missed out or received less than others. That happens in every family, but the potential is great in stepfamilies.

a. If, somewhere along the way, you missed out on that blessing, how did that affect you?

b. How might your life have been different had you received all five elements of The Blessing?

c. If you were to extend that blessing to your children, how might that affect your parenting style and results?

10. Reflect on your own desire to extend God's blessing through you to your extended family. How might you express the character of God through:

a. meaningful touch?

b. spoken words?

c. expressing high value?

d. picturing a special future for the one being blessed?

e. an active commitment to see the blessing come to pass?

11. What is something of spiritual significance that you could put in your "last will and testament," to pass the blessing on to your children in a way that is appropriate for each one? In the space below, write out their names and a different blessing for each one. Time permitting, pray about these concerns in your group or with one other person outside group time, someone who knows your family situation.

12. Suppose your children got a sneak preview of your actual last will and testament. Would any one of them have reason for concluding that you were playing favorites? How so?

Have you seen favoritism in your own parenting? If so, what changes would you like to make? (Would you change your will? Would you somehow make up for emotional deficits in your child's bank account with you? If you woke up tomorrow and found you were suddenly parenting with more effectiveness and less bias, what exactly would be different?)

The Rest of the Story

Part of Jacob's life that was skipped over in the above study deserves at least passing mention. This story illustrates the "children-learn-what-they-live" principle. It also has a silver lining that endears this patriarch of blended families to those of us who struggle with similar relationship issues.

By "silver lining," I am referring to the silver cup placed and found in Benjamin's sack (Genesis 44:1-13). At Joseph's direction, his servant planted the cup, making Benjamin appear to be a thief. This led to a much-needed family reunion. The "theft" provided a pretext for Joseph to entrap and humiliate Jacob's family. Then, later on, he reconciled with all of them. Read Genesis 42-47 for "the rest of the story" and chapter 50:15-21 for the recap.

The good news in all Jacob's upbringing and fathering, partisan as it was, is simply this: *A patriarch can pass along the blessing to his sons and grandsons because (and to the extent that) he himself has received the blessing from his father.* Jacob was blessed to be a blessing in turn, as was his father Abraham (Genesis 12:2-3).

Our Next "Dad of the Week"

The story of Jacob and his sons is not the only example of a partisan parent highlighted in the Bible. Several generations later, in the period of the Judges, we pick up the sorry story of an ancient promise keeper who faced a conflict with his daughter because of a rash vow to the Lord.

In preparation for this next chapter on fathering, read Judges 10:6—12:7 (about Jephthah), together with Luke 8:40-42,49-56 (about Jairus). Then reflect on what it means to be one of those "Warrior Fathers" caught in a classic conflict between faithfulness to work, to one's God, and to one's family. The outcome is both heroic and ironic for the daughters of these two working men, Jephthah and Jairus, who live out very different father-daughter priorities.

Endnotes

1. See Gary Smalley, *The Blessing* (Pocket Books, New York: 1990) for an exposition and application of these five elements.

2. For a prototype of this, see Figures I and II, pages 22-23.

—•••—

A child's suffering can be very real and very deep and all the worse since a child has neither the wisdom nor the resources of mature men and women. . . . Those people who think of adolescence as a happy, care-free time either possess deficient emotions or inadequate memories."

Louis Bromfield (1896-1956)

—•••—

"The injuries we do and those we suffer
are seldom weighed in the same scales."

Aesop (around 550 B.C.)

—•••—

"In every pang that rends the heart
The Man of Sorrows had a part."

Michael Bruce

—•••—

"A good father will leave his imprint on his daughter for the rest of her life."

James C. Dobson (1936-)

—•••—

CHAPTER THREE

Jephthah, Jairus and Other Warrior Fathers: Sacrificing Your Daughter for a Mission *or* Sacrificing Everything for Your Daughter

While I am not the father of a daughter, I ask that you not discount what I say in this chapter about father-daughter relationships. I will speak mostly as a reporter and from the biblical accounts of Jephthah and Jairus. Jephthah and Jairus are two fathers who both enjoyed and grieved the father-daughter relationship, but in different ways. As we shall see, Jephthah and Jairus reacted differently to the possibility of the sudden and tragic end of their relationship with their respective daughters.

The other angle pursued in profiling these two fathers is the dilemma we fathers face in honoring promises to our work, when to do so conflicts with our family's needs. If you are like Jephthah, you will sacrifice even your only daughter for the sake of a mission. But if you are like Jairus, you will sacrifice everything for your daughter.

Jephthah's Sacrifice of His Daughter

Jephthah was the warrior-judge who lost his daughter, an only child, through his own zealous devotion to work over family. His family background may explain how his family came to be viewed as secondary, even expedient, in relation to keeping his commitments at work.

Jephthah the Gileadite was born of a prostitute, rejected unjustly by his half-brothers, and grew up a social outcast (Judges 11:1-2). Sibling rivalry and multiple parents evidently bore bad fruit in this blended family. Whereas in Jacob's family, the son of a favorite wife is the one despised by his half-brothers (Genesis 37), in Gilead's family, the opposite is true: the son of a prostitute is despised by his half-brothers.

Rejected by family and driven from his father's house (Judges 11:7), Jephthah hit the road at an early age. For the rest of his youth, he had no father to mentor him and no place to call home. Hence, Jephthah joined a roving band of mercenary "adventurers" (11:3) and soon became their gang leader. Boys with absentee dads have often joined alternative families for the recognition and belonging that only a true father can provide.

To erase the pain and rise above the troubled circumstances of his illegitimate birth and hostile upbringing, Jephthah agreed to become the head warrior and judge of Israel (11:6-11). Perhaps, he reasoned, such an appointment would earn long-denied acceptance from family and peers.

This strong deal-maker and brilliant military strategist (11:12-28) backed up his talk with action. That, and his prayerful dependence on God, brought him success (11:29). In gratitude to God, Jephthah foolishly vowed to sacrifice the first thing that came out of his house (11:30-31). Much to his horror, that "first thing" was his daughter (11:34-35).

That Jephthah would go through with his vow to the Lord is, on one level, a commendable act of integrity. But, on another and higher level, the thought that Jephthah would actually sacrifice his only daughter to keep his promise—or that the Lord would even hold him to that rash vow—is horrifying and incomprehensible.[1]

Could Jephthah be one of those despicable child-killers?

Child sacrifice was a pagan rite practiced by neighboring Middle Eastern peoples. Yet it was contrary to everything the Jewish religion stands for.[2] Hence, some interpreters think Jephthah could not possibly have followed through with his vow to slay his daughter and present her as a burnt offering.

Could Jephthah be one of those despicable child-killers? Or did he only set his daughter apart as a virgin for the rest of her life? The text simply says, "He did to her as he had vowed. And she was a virgin" (11:39). Either choice cut off Jephthah's hope for a descendant.

Lest we judge Jephthah as too crude or rash to emulate, let us remember that he went on to lead Israel six more years (Judges 12:1-7) and emerged as a man of faith, revered by Jews and Christians alike (1 Samuel 12:11; Hebrews 11:32). How so?

Perhaps Jephthah hoped an animal would have come out of his house first, not his daughter. When going ahead with plans to make a human sacrifice, perhaps he hoped all along God would provide a substitute, even a lamb or goat, as He did for Abraham and Isaac (Genesis 22).

The Gabra chief sacrifices his daughter

The Cushitic Gabra, a tribe of nomadic and monotheistic people on the Kenya-Ethiopian frontier, had never heard of Abraham or Jesus, but in their oral history they tell this story of sacrifice that prepared them for the Gospel:[3]

> Many generations ago, the tragic, accidental death of one tribal chief's son at the hands of the other chief's family shattered the decades-long peace and friendship. An "eye for an eye" and "life for a life" was the law of the land. So the two parties mutually, but reluctantly, agreed that the offending tribe's chief would offer his daughter in payment for the dead boy. Only another child's life could satisfy the just demands of the law and keep an equitable peace, even if that meant the chief's eldest daughter must die.
>
> The date for the sacrifice was set, and the daughter left in an enclosed thicket of thorns. She was guarded by warriors and would be sacrificed at dawn. The next morning, when the two chiefs returned to do the inevitable human sacrifice, they were astounded to find the girl sleeping peacefully, clutching a lamb in her arms. It was a yearling, a "lamb without blemish." The two chiefs asked of their god, "What could this possibly mean?" They concluded that the chief's daughter had been spared and that their god had provided a substitute as compensation of "life for a life."

Such are the mysterious ways of the sovereign and merciful God, the God of Abraham and Isaac, of Jephthah and his daughter. Had Jephthah found such a substitute, our biblical story would have a happier ending. As it is, Jephthah's daughter had Isaac-like faith. She affirmed the priority of Jephthah keeping his promise to God, even if that meant she would die without ever marrying (11:37-38).

This father's story is fraught with contradictions: The ultimate child abuse is perpetuated by a faithful promise-keeper; human sacrifice is (perhaps) committed by a revered man of integrity, in violation of God's clear prohibition. The fate of Jephthah's daughter is commemorated by Jewish girls to this day. And this gruesome story is recorded in inspired Scripture for Christian fathers to somehow profit from.

Learning from Jephthah's dilemma

Being banished from home for his scandalous birth and rejected by his peers may explain Jephthah's need to make a man of himself. In several settings where rogues sometimes excel—among fellow adventurers, at the negotiating table with enemies, and on the battlefield where violent behavior is rewarded—his brilliant military record gained him the acceptance that eluded him since childhood.

Let us fathers take care how we show disapproval and discipline to our children, especially to stepchildren, lest they conclude with Jephthah, "Didn't you hate me and drive me from my father's house?" (11:7).

Whatever the reasons behind Jephthah's rash vow, he paid for his actions—just as fathers throughout history have lost their children when vows at work conflict with vows at home. This story illustrates the double bind many men feel between the call of work and family. Many "warrior fathers" and men of integrity, zealous to uphold their work and their word at all costs, make the same mistake Jephthah did.

We can empathize with his dilemma by remembering that many fathers break promises to their family. We conveniently forget our girl's piano recital or our boy's baseball game for a "prior commitment" (another business meeting, a game of golf or men's night out). Workaholics ask their family to understand that work must come first. Military men put "God and country" above family. So also Jephthah. He loved God and responded to the call of people who pressed him into military service. . .but forgot the welfare of his own family.

Fortunately, not all dads choose as he did. The story of Jairus has a happier ending. This time, the daughter comes back from the dead!

JAIRUS'S SACRIFICE FOR HIS DAUGHTER

Jairus was the president of a local synagogue. He was in charge of ordering worship services and maintaining discipline in that faith community. When his daughter became dangerously ill, this distinguished ruler could have simply sent for Jesus. He could have quietly dispatched a servant, or even used his considerable influence to "require" Jesus' presence. Instead, Jairus dropped all pretense, ran to Jesus, broke through the crowd, and, in front of everyone, prostrated himself before the Great Physician (Luke 8:40-41).

Jairus knelt, begging Jesus to heal his twelve-year-old daughter, who was dying (8:42). Indeed, by the time Jesus arrived, she had been pronounced "dead" (8:49). The distraught father, in abject humility and vulnerability, admitted there was something his daughter needed that he could not give her, something that Jesus alone could provide.

The story takes on new meaning if we examine it from the daughter's vantage point.[4] Imagine a girl, twelve years old, on the threshold of womanhood. She believes, rather naively, *As long as Daddy is with me, everything will work out fine. Daddy has all the power.* But when she is dying and dad, the synagogue ruler, is ultimately powerless to help, her faith in him could be shattered. She loses something—her image of an all-wise, all-powerful, all-good father who can make it all right. That image of her father slips away, along with her health. Perhaps she thinks, *Daddy cannot save me. He is not my Savior. Daddy is only human, after all.*

Most kids discover their daddy's failings long before age twelve, but the point remains useful. Stay with me for argument's sake. Who of us have not felt our humanity confirmed in the experience of parenting and failing to deliver as expected or promised? Who of us have labored and anguished, as did Jairus, for a child in dire straits, only to come up short?

Happily, this daughter and father did come to place their faith in Jesus, who alone has the power to make all people whole. We have much to learn from their faith.

Learning from Jairus's dilemma

There comes a point in our careers, often in mid-life, when we realize we will never be the president of the company, mayor of the city, or author of a best-selling novel. Such men in mid-life crisis often comfort themselves with the thought they can at least be "president" of their daughter's life. And so we take control, do our best by her, and only reluctantly let go or admit we can't do it all for our beloved. At some point we must commit her to the hands of God.

Only in her darkest hour of suffering did Jairus's daughter experience the resurrection power of the Lord Jesus. Just when the prognosis was most bleak, Jairus's faith was rewarded and his daughter healed. So also with us. It is often darkest before the dawn—that is both the bad news and the good news. In suffering, we learn to appreciate what God's Son endured for us. As the early church father Augustine once said, "God had one Son on earth without sin, but never one without suffering."

God knows a father's grief, as He allowed His own Son to suffer and die. Yet often we want to shield our loved ones from experiencing any hurt. We want to interfere and take it upon ourselves to be our child's savior. That's when God may push us out of the picture, so that the child may experience firsthand God's own gracious presence and power.

Questions for Group Warm-up

These get-acquainted questions can be answered without reading the thematic introduction or doing the Bible study for this chapter.

1. What do you find special about little girls, especially your daughters or nieces?

- ☐ Her ability to sing, dance, or perform for her parents.
- ☐ The things she makes, draws, or writes for me.
- ☐ The things she does to help around the house.
- ☐ Her skill and performance level in school or in athletics.
- ☐ The way she admires me and brags about me to her friends.
- ☐ The pride I feel when she's all dressed up in her party best.
- ☐ She admires boys and measures them against me.
- ☐ Other (please explain):

2. On your school playground, in your teen years, or in your adventurous young adult years, who did you count on to bail you out when you got into trouble? (Were you ever called on to be that hero in action?)

- ☐ The Big Bully on the block.
- ☐ The Big Man On Campus.
- ☐ A big brother at home.
- ☐ Mom or Dad, when I needed a financial bail-out.
- ☐ The bailiff in jail, or attorney in court.
- ☐ Other (please explain):

Questions for Bible Study

Read Judges 10:6—12:7. Then continue your group study by individually answering these questions and sharing with others from your notes.

3. Jephthah was the "mighty warrior" of his day with a rogue following and abilities to negotiate for peace and strategize for victory. Who in our era do you see as a Jephthah-type "mighty warrior" (and why)?

- ☐ Henry Kissinger (a studious deal-maker).
- ☐ Jimmy Carter (a studious peacemaker).
- ☐ Robert E. Lee or George Patton (a brilliant military strategist).
- ☐ Robin Hood (a bit roguish but still a good guy).
- ☐ Rambo (a blood-and-guts patriot who loved God-and-country).
- ☐ Other (please explain):

What do you see in the biblical record (11:12-29) that indicates Jephthah was a strong deal-maker, peacemaker, and military strategist, capable of defeating the dreaded Ammonites?

4. What reasons did Jephthah have for trusting God to help him defeat an ominous enemy he had never faced?

5. What was this ancient promise keeper thinking . . .

a. when he first made his vow (11:30-31)?

b. when he realized who came out of his home to greet him (11:34-35)?

c. when "he did to her as he had vowed" (11:39)?

6. As incomprehensible and reprehensible as child sacrifice is to Jews and Christians alike, how do you account for Jephthah's (apparent) sacrifice of his daughter?

- ☐ He was a man of integrity and had to keep his word.
- ☐ His violent streak may be accounted for by the meanness and rejection of his home environment.
- ☐ Military men always put God and country above their family.
- ☐ He thought God would relieve him of keeping his promise or would provide a substitute sacrifice.
- ☐ He was caught in a genuine double-bind, a no-win conflict between work and family; he made the best choice he could.
- ☐ I don't know; there is no way to justify such ultimate abuse.
- ☐ Other (please explain):

Read Luke 8:40-42,49-56. Then continue your group study by individually answering these questions and sharing from your notes with others.

7. What was going through the mind of Jairus and/or his daughter . . .

a. when they realized Jairus could do nothing more to heal her (8:40-42)?

b. when Jairus got word his daughter had died (8:49)?

c. when Jesus said, "Don't be afraid, just believe, and she will be healed" (8:50)?

8. Jairus saw his daughter brought back from the dead; Jephthah did not. How do you account for the different outcomes?

- ☐ Men of integrity keep their word and give their children up to God, with no strings attached; God will do what He wills.
- ☐ Faith in God does not work magic and guarantees nothing.
- ☐ God prefers religious guys over military men.
- ☐ One daughter had a choice and willingly became a martyr.
- ☐ Jesus was present in one scene, absent in the other.

- ☐ Jairus did the harder thing for a proud father and humbled himself; Jephthah did not, but stubbornly stayed the course.
- ☐ Other (please explain):

Questions for Application

This third set of questions is designed to bring the point home to yourself and other fathers.

9. Jephthah's daughter was granted a two-month lease on life "to roam the hills and weep with [her] friends" (11:37). Jairus' daughter also lived under a death sentence. If you knew you had only a short time (two months) to live, how would you spend that time? (Why not live that way the rest of your life, anyway?)

10. What memorable promise, kept or broken, has significantly shaped who you are today? This can be a promise made by your own father on behalf of his family, or one you have made yourself. Share your promise.

- ☐ It was a promise broken in deference to other priorities.
- ☐ It was a promise waffled on, keeping with the low status of vows in society.
- ☐ It was a promise kept with faith, despite its unpopularity.
- ☐ It was a promise broken, because to keep it would be sin.
- ☐ Other (please explain):

11. In light of this case study, how do you honor your promises to your work and family, especially when the two appear to be in direct conflict?

- ☐ I'm like Jephthah, inclined to sacrifice family for the sake of mission, especially at crunch time when deadlines are pressing; I keep those work vows even when it costs my family.
- ☐ I'm like Jairus, inclined to sacrifice everything—including pride of accomplishment or promotions at work—for my family, even if it costs me my job.

Describe to the other men in your group those heartaches and unresolved conflicts between family and work. Be brief and specific. Time permitting, pray about those issues.

The Rest of the Story

The stories of these two fathers and their daughters are not the only biblical examples of warriors and promise keepers whose crises of faith center around their daughters.

Jacob's family come to the rescue of Dinah (Genesis 34); Job lost his three daughters (Job 1); Mordecai fosters courageous faith in his adopted Esther (see Chapter 10).

Our Next "Dad of the Week"

The next father we profile is a well-intentioned dad who helps to raise up a judge to lead God's people. This father also stakes his faith in a special, unshakable promise to God. By a Nazirite vow, Manoah promises to raise his son Samson with a spiritual head start. In preparation for this next chapter on fathering, read Judges 13:1—14:4, plus Numbers 6:1-21. Then reflect on what it means to want God's best for your child.

Endnotes

1. One instance where the Lord releases someone from an "irrevocable" vow to keep a higher commitment to family is when he confronts the issue of *Corban* (Mark 7:9-13). Faith pledges should be set aside to meet special family needs.

2. See Leviticus 18:21; Deuteronomy 18:10; 2 Kings 3:27; 16:3; 17:17-18; 21:6; 23:10; Jeremiah 7:31; 32:35.)

3. Adapted and used with permission from a sermon preached at High Point Church, Madison, Wis., by Dick Robinson, recounting his brother Paul's anthropological research. Paul Robinson now works with MAP International.

4. For this insight, I am indebted to an October 1993 sermon preached by Gordon Dalbey at High Point Church, Madison, Wis.

—•••—

I owe more to the fire and the hammer and file than to anything else in my Lord's workshop. I sometimes question whether I have learned anything except through the rod. When my schoolroom is darkened, I see most."
Charles Haddon Spurgeon (1834-1892)

—•••—

"It does not take great men to do great things; it only takes consecrated men."
Phillips Brooks (1835-1893)

—•••—

"Consecration is not wrapping one's self in a holy web in the sanctuary and then coming forth after prayer and twilight meditation and saying, 'There, I am consecrated.' Consecration is going out into the world where God Almighty is and using every power for his glory. It is taking all advantages as trust funds."
Henry Ward Beecher(1813-1887)

—•••—

"God wills the development of all men. When from time to time he makes them hear his call to self-denial, to renunciation and even self-sacrifice, it is not for their impoverishment but for their enrichment. . . . All Christ's calls to detachment are accompanied by promises that point to their real meaning."
Paul Tournier (1898-1986)

—•••—

CHAPTER FOUR

Manoah and Other Well-Intentioned "Rule-Book" Dads: Wanting God's Best for Your Child's Life & Work

Rearing children by the book, even the Good Book—or a good tape or a parenting workshop—is the goal of many parents. (Perhaps this is true even for some of you reading this book.) A bookstore survey recently touted 430 titles available on child-rearing for those parents who want to do it "by the book." Add to that list every other available self-help resource—the audio tapes, video seminars, weekly radio talk shows, newspaper columns, and support groups—and you get the picture.

With all the self-help resources and rules geared to help parents, it's a wonder how the previous "unenlightened" generation ever got along without them! Manoah is another dad looking for a "rule" that will help him develop a man out of his son. A heavenly resource provided one.

Rearing Children by the Book

Where would we be without parenting books? One possible answer: Maybe some of us wouldn't be here today if our parents had read enough to know what they were getting into *before* having kids!

Manoah wanted to be a father; he and his wife just couldn't conceive (Judges 13:2). Not until the Lord solved their infertility problem could they conceive. An angel announced they'd soon be having a son.

Then, another dilemma faced the once-childless Manoah. He feared he did not know enough to be a good father. (Who of us *ever* knows enough?) After years of childlessness, he and his wife were promised a child and, like any first-time-around parent, Manoah wanted to know more than just the due date. He wanted to know, "What is to be the *rule* for this boy's life and work?" (Judges 13:12, italics mine).

Manoah is not alone. Conscientious parents still ask this question and read up on discipline, motivation and follow-through. It is easier to rear children solely "by the book." Many parents, authors, and publishers evidently think highly principled, parenting-by-formula is possible. How else do you justify the current maze of parenting self-help books?

WHAT RULE BOOK WOULD HELP YOU RAISE A SON LIKE CAIN OR SAMSON—OR CALVIN?

No wonder some of the ancients—the biblical Cain, for example—turned out so badly; those parents raising a little Cain didn't have a book on child psychology to read. Manoah, who would have had his hands full raising Samson by *any* rule of discipline, reminds me of a recent Calvin and Hobbes cartoon strip. This one depicted Calvin's dad seated in his reading chair, perusing one of those 430 self-help parenting books. That, of course, piques Calvin's curiosity. But the father denies his son the opportunity to read the book he's reading. In the punch line, he glibly shrugs off Calvin, saying, in effect: "Sorry, kid, this is one of those books you're not allowed to read until it's too late."

I suspect it's also "too late" for most of you reading this book. For anyone already a father, it's *too late* to undo that first passage of parenting. If your kids are full-grown, another "too-little-too-late" rule book will not help. But if you have a child in his or her formative years, one whose Christian character and moral compass still needs a set point, you will get much out of this chapter. And if you aspire to have a profound father-like influence on others' children during their formative years, you will also profit from a more in-depth look at Manoah.

This ancient prototype of a promise keeper and well-intentioned, "strictly-by-the-book" dad made a vow that offered a spiritual head start to his son Samson. It was a called a Nazirite's vow. Thanks, in part, to this parental pledge for God's best, Samson was in a position to deliver the Israelites in a mighty way—but not before breaking every rule set down for him by his dad. But that's getting ahead of our story. Let's first take a closer look at this vow.

THE NAZIRITE'S VOW OF ABSTINENCE AND CONSECRATION

Samson's parents dedicated him to the Lord, in fulfillment of the Nazirite's vow (Judges 13:4-5). According to the Law of Moses, the Nazirite vow of separation obliged one to abstain from consuming any drink made from grapes (Numbers 6:3-4). Though intoxication by the priests or lay leaders may have been a problem back then, this was not the real issue here. The grapes and strong drink represented temptations of the worldly culture which the man of God was to avoid at all costs.

The father who makes a similar voluntary vow today may do so because he fears alcoholism. Abstinence from alcohol may also keep temptation from others who might be predisposed that way. A third motivation might be a desire to withhold support of the beer and wine industry which contributes indirectly to alcohol-related accidents and crimes.

The typical Nazirite also abstained from shaving. Uncut hair was a sign of unimpaired strength. After a limited period of time, the Nazirite would be free to cut his hair, but the cuttings were offered to the Lord as a further sign of his consecration (Numbers 6:18). Both John the Baptist (Luke 1:15; Matthew 11:18-19) and Paul (Acts 18:18) had taken *Nazirite* vows, as did Hannah on Samuel's behalf (1 Samuel 1:11). The Nazirites were a consecrated class of men, set aside like the prophets for special use by God in calling people to faithfulness (Amos 2:11).

The vow also obliged the Nazirite to never touch a corpse, nor to go near a dead body. This was a ceremonial uncleanness the Nazirite was to avoid at all costs, even at family funerals (Numbers 6:7). The exceptional Nazirite, like Samson, also vowed not to eat anything "unclean." All food had to be kosher, that is, consecrated according to Jewish custom (Judges 13:4,7). This vow was incumbent on the parents, as well as the son, in Manoah's family.

Nazirite vows could be limited to the formative years, or to special periods of consecration (Numbers 6:13). The vow was taken in order to concentrate mental, physical, and spiritual energies for a particular task to which the Lord was calling the individual. In the case of Samson, the calling to be a "Nazirite to God" was "since birth," or permanent (Judges 16:17). In taking this vow on behalf of Samson, the well-intentioned Manoah did not know, nor did he try to determine, the life direction his son would choose. Yet Manoah did his best to prepare Samson with a "rule" applicable to whatever path he would eventually take.

A Son's Broken Vows and a Dad's Broken Heart

Samson eventually broke this vow taken on his behalf by the promise-keeping Manoah. Samson first broke his dad's heart by marrying a non-Jewish Philistine. It was lust at first sight; marriage was an afterthought (Judges 14:1-8).

Then Samson touched the decaying carcass and ate honey from the innards of the lion he had killed (14:6-9). Samson must have known he was breaking two aspects of the Nazirite's vow, for he purposely kept this incident from his parents. In further rebellion, Samson threw a drinking party for thirty buddies and invited his dad. This party had to include wine; so it seems Samson broke another part of his vow (14:10-11).

How like a rebel son to cover up his transgression from an unknowing father! That reminds me of the days when I used to take my dad's car—against his explicit wishes (while my parents were away)—and disguise the misdeed by resetting the odometer. Other times I drank beer as an underage teen and disguised my breath with mints. On another occasion I even helped to arrange a beer-drinking bash for thirty companions of my brother Bill, all at my parents' house. Mom and Dad were *not* invited, but later found out.

When the rebel Samson told Delilah (who told the Philistines) that the secret of his superhuman strength was in his unshaven hair (16:17-20), we see another Nazirite vow broken. Not only did his strength leave him then, but worse; "he did not know the Lord had left him."

Despite Samson's waywardness, he was used mightily by God. He acted to free the Israelites from the dreaded Philistines (14:4,19; 15:14-15; 16:28-30). This happened just as the angel had promised Manoah and his wife before Samson's birth (13:5). See "The Rest of the Story."

Learning from Manoah's Vow and Samson's "Rule"

Manoah did not know the precise plans or "rule" God had for his son. How differently we would all parent if we knew what our sons and daughters were destined to become! But God rarely works that way. And if He did routinely give us the advance scoop, the parenting job still would be overwhelming. Imagine, for example, how overwhelming it was for Joseph to be told, "You are to give him the name Jesus because he will save his people from their sins" (Matthew 1:21). Imagine being overshadowed by a son with such a destiny and the awesome parental duties it entailed! (See Chapter 10, "Joseph and Other Neglected Stepfathers.")

Although Manoah very much wanted to know the angel's intentions for his son, he had to be content with knowing only that his son had a guardian angel and that God had a plan for Samson. Manoah knew only enough to rear his son in an orthodox rule-book tradition—and that was good enough for God's purposes.

Still, I wonder if Samson's rebelliousness could have been avoided. His broken vows bore bad fruit, but even more harmful was the broken father-son relationship. Perhaps Manoah fathered by rules instead of a heart-to-heart relationship. There's even more to the enigmatic Manoah-Samson story than meets the eye. Let's investigate.

Questions for Group Warm-up

These get-acquainted questions can be answered without reading the thematic introduction or doing the Bible study for this chapter.

1. Choose one of the following "bad hair" stories that will produce a chuckle or even regale your group with laughter. If your story helps introduce one theme of our study, so much the better.

  a. Recall what you looked like in your younger days. Compare your youthful hairstyle with those you see on your own sons or nephews. How have hair styles changed since your youth?

b. When was your hair the shortest, the longest, or the kinkiest?

c. Can you picture yourself with a shaved head? (Perhaps you were shorn of your hair—and your individuality—in the army, in prison, fraternity hazing, by a religious cult, or in the hospital.) What was that like?

d. Can you picture yourself going bald? (Perhaps you have the male pattern baldness from your mom's dad.) What would you (or have you) done to rectify that situation?

e. Alternately, what do you think you'd look like with very long hair or unshaven facial hair? (What would your family and your corporate culture think of the Samson-look? Would someone think you were trying to edge out Fabio for the front cover of a romance novel?)

Questions for Bible Study

Read Numbers 6:1-21 and Judges 13:16. Then continue your group study by individually answering these questions and sharing with others from your notes.

2. After learning he'd finally have a son, how does Manoah behave (13:8-23) and why?

- ☐ Manoah was behaving like any over-anxious, first-time parent who wanted all the answers.
- ☐ When told of the boy's destiny, Manoah was overwhelmed by the prospect of raising up and training such a savior.
- ☐ Manoah wanted the messenger to hang around for dinner, fellowship and worship, as he was fearful of spiritual things.
- ☐ The angel represented a dimension of life which the rational, level-headed Manoah could neither understand nor control.
- ☐ Other (please explain):

3. Why do you suppose the angel asked the parents, specifically Manoah's wife, to join their son in keeping the Nazirite's vow of abstinence from alcohol and "unclean" food (Judges 13:7,13-14)?

- ☐ The angel knew about the *fetal-alcohol syndrome* and wanted the mother to give birth to a healthy baby.
- ☐ The angel knew the importance of *parental* role-modeling, rule-setting, and promise-keeping for the family that seeks to raise up godly children.

☐ The angel didn't know what he was talking about.
☐ While in Old Testament times it was the father's role to bring up his children to know and love God, the angel knew Samson's mother would be needed for this area of spiritual discipline.
☐ Other (please explain):

4. What do you make of this husband-wife, father-mother team?

☐ The wife was the more devout, spiritually sensitive one.
☐ Manoah was the more level-headed, go-by-the-rule-book parent.
☐ The two made a great pair, complementing one's ruling passion with the other's passion for rules.
☐ Samson needed a guardian angel for this scheme to ever work.
☐ Other (please explain):

5. Every strength, every virtue, and every rule has its flip side. So it was with Samson and Manoah. While Samson had great physical strength and a spiritual head-start, what was he missing?

☐ The rules got in way of a relationship with his dad.
☐ The rules were administered without a sense of ultimate purpose, so that Samson's religion became nothing more than do's and don'ts.
☐ "Casting pearls before swine" (or teaching wisdom) is no use with a rebellious, hot-headed, hot-blooded fool like Samson.
☐ Manoah let his wife do most of the spiritual nurturing and disciplining, but Samson needed a more actively involved dad.
☐ Samson took the rule of God and the power of His Spirit for granted; he did not follow his parents' model of humility and gratitude.
☐ Samson experienced the Holy Spirit only as an intermittent touch, not as an abiding presence.
☐ Samson needed a good, trustworthy woman.
☐ Samson needed a men's group to hold him accountable for his sin.
☐ Other (please explain):

Questions for Application

This third set of questions is designed to bring the point home to yourself and other fathers.

6. When it became apparent that you'd soon become a parent, what did you do to prepare yourself?

☐ I read everything I could get my hands on.
☐ I listened to my mother's advice and other "old wives' tales."

- ☐ I went to Lamaze and other parent-support classes.
- ☐ I let my wife do most of the child-rearing after I planted the seed.
- ☐ I appealed to all the guardian angels and patron saints I knew—anyone who would help me with this humanly impossible, divinely difficult task.
- ☐ Other (please explain):

7. Manoah wanted to know how to raise Samson to fulfill his God- given destiny. But as Calvin's dad jokes, if we knew beforehand what the job of parenting entails, we might not accept the assignment. Knowing what you know now, and seeing your child(ren)'s progress, what would you do differently if you had to do it over again? (Answer each part of this question, a through h.)

a. I'd have our kids earlier/later/not at all, because: ____________________.

b. I'd have more/less/the same number of kids, because: ________________.

c. I'd have more/less/no rules to live by, especially in the area of: __________.

d. I'd give up smoking/drinking/drugs/other: ________________________.

e. I'd have an adult-teen talk about alcohol/sex/marriage/other: __________.

f. In my spiritual parenting next time around, I'd try: _________________.

g. I'd take "guardian angels" seriously, enlist their help with: _____________.

h. I'd raise my child to develop and use his natural bent, spiritual gift or personal strength in: ______________.

8. Some say that if you *always* correct a child's behavior, urging conformity to some pre-set rules for Christian kids, or if you *only* fill their minds with Christian doctrine and values, the chances are high they will one day rebel, as did Samson. Others say the opposite, that an *unbending* application of the rules is what guarantees that a child will grow to respect God's law and will *not* depart from it (Proverbs 22:6). Still others say, never mind the rules, that a close father-son *relationship* is what increases the likelihood of that child growing up to serve the Lord. What do *you* think?

9. What goals did your dad have regarding your "life and work?"

- ☐ I was groomed and expected to take over the family business.
- ☐ My parents wanted me to excel in school and become a "doctor, lawyer, or Indian chief."
- ☐ My parents dedicated me to God, expecting me to be a missionary or priest.
- ☐ I was reared in the ways of God and was expected to do all to His glory, no matter what career or marriage I ended up in.
- ☐ I was reared with a multiplicity of options and no particular spiritual direction or expectations.
- ☐ Other (please explain):

10. What goals did (do) you have for your firstborn regarding his or her "life and work?" (Did, or do, you pass along your father's expectations or live vicariously through your firstborn's accomplishments?)

11. As time and trust level in your group permits, share these parental vows or expectations for yourself and your children. Pray for one another about keeping and fulfilling them—in God's way, with God's strength.

The Rest of the Story

Despite being consecrated to God by his parents, Samson rebelled. He departed from their good intentions and their rule book. We like to think of Samson as used by God to humble and slay the Philistines. We don't like to think that this man of God had difficulty in keeping his raging male hormones in check, or that he could not control his angry, vengeful, and abusive impulses. Sexual abstinence, delayed gratification, self-control, and anger-management were not his strong suits.

The lusty, hot-tempered, vow-breaking Samson presents an enigma. His limited virtues and obvious vices belie the fact that he is counted a hero of faith (Hebrews 11:32). This Hercules-like hero avenged himself and delivered the Israelites from the dominating, pagan Philistines. Single-handedly and by the Spirit's power (14:19; 15:14; 16:28), he confounded them with riddles, burned their fields with foxes set afire, used and abused three of their women, and slayed a thousand of their men with the jawbone of a donkey.

Although he frequently acted like a man out of control, he did eventually settle down to become more than God's man of the hour; Samson "led" or judged Israel for *twenty* years (15:20; 16:31). At his death, when he toppled the temple, he took more Philistines with him than he killed during his lifetime.

The story of Manoah's dedicated but strong-willed son-turned-savior shows that kids will go their own way, but can still do good—thanks in part to the spiritual head start their well-intentioned fathers (and mothers) provide them. Yet Samson's parents must have agonized for years, not knowing how their son would turn out. Samson was buried in Manoah's tomb (16:31), indicating that Manoah predeceased his son. Let us hope this well-intentioned rule-book dad got to see Samson lead Israel for some part of his twenty-year tenure. If not, then Manoah shares common ground with many dads who die before seeing the fulfillment of their fathering.

Our Next "Dad of the Week"

Our next chapter on fathering also focuses on a son who was consecrated for the Lord's service with a Nazirite's life-long vow. But this consecrated "Nazirite of God" turned out much different than Samson. In preparation for this next chapter on fathering, read 1 Samuel 1—4. Then reflect on what it means to be a "Delinquent Dad"—one who succeeds with a foster son while failing to discipline his own two sons.

—•••—

"A stern discipline pervades all nature, which is a little cruel that it may be very kind."
Edmund Spencer (1552-1599)

—•••—

"It is one thing to praise discipline; another to submit to it."
Miguel de Cervantes (1547-1616)

—•••—

"Build me a son, O Lord, who will be strong enough to know when he is weak and brave enough to face himself when he is afraid, one who will be proud and unbending in honest defeat and humble and gentle in victory."
Douglas MacArthur (1880-1964)

—•••—

CHAPTER FIVE

Eli and Other Delinquent Dads: Heeding God's Discipline for Those in Your Charge

Many dads would agree that maintaining consistent and fair discipline in the home is their number one concern. Conscientious fathers have always wrestled with how strict or lax to be with rules and chores. Foster parents, who must develop rules, limits, and expectations for street-smart, violence-prone foster kids, *will* struggle, especially with this firmness and fairness issue. So will parents in blended families. This is also true for intact families with large spaces between kids; treating older and younger siblings even-handedly can be tricky.

You get the picture. Maintaining consistent discipline over all those placed in our charge means that we make every effort to avoid double standards for all our children: "his" and "her" biological kids, older-younger kids, foster kids, even the adults. (We can't very well maintain a rule like "no interrupting someone else while they're talking" if that's what we ourselves do.)

The Great Discipline Debate

Baby Boomer and Buster fathers are more conversant than their fathers were in the discipline debate. Our generation knows much about the ways children grow, learn, and feel. Hence, we know enough not to strap kids with a label ("You are a slob") or a self-fulfilling prophecy ("You'll never amount to much"). We've been taught to describe the behavior we don't like ("You did not make your bed") or, more positively, the alternative outcome we want ("I like clean rooms"). Today's dads generally know to differentiate between the *feelings* and *behavior* of their children ("It's okay to be angry, but it's not okay to hit your sister"). And we try not to harp on the negative but "catch our kids doing something good" and praise them for that.

We have come to recognize bothersome behaviors typical of certain developmental stages. We are thankful those behaviors are self-correcting with gentle support and guidance from us. As a result, today's dad will first *listen* to needs and *ask* questions, *request* instead of demand, *explain* reasons rather than bark orders, and *contract* for changed behavior.

The old authoritarian, punishment-focused model ("Do as I say, or else!") has been abused. Some children are beaten or abandoned and need protective services. As a result of documented research, media hype and celebrated court cases of physical and emotional abuse of children, our society has declared war on child abuse.

But this does not mean we modern dads jump on the "dare-not- do-anything-to-traumatize-my-precious-darling" bandwagon. That is, not if we're reading our Bibles and learning from our biblical forefathers, and not if we've learned anything from social science and family counselors.

Delinquency: Not Just a Kid's Problem

Delinquent or lax and neglectful fathers contribute to the delinquency of their kids.[1] Through neglect and leniency, we rob our children of the security of knowing we are there for them. Neglect can wound or close their spirit by withholding emotional access from them. Inconsistency or passivity in applying rules and limits can breed acting-out behavior in children. An overly permissive and neglectful dad will find himself saying:

"Well, okay, you can stay up to watch one more show."

"Please don't get angry, you know I don't want a scene."

"Can't you see I'm busy right now? Get lost!"

"That's your problem. I've got other things to do."

If you are tempted to look the other way when your child consciously disobeys, you are not alone. Another lax father, little-known outside ancient Israel, is Eli. He was the Hebrew priest and father figure who raised the boy Samuel to be a prophet in the Lord's service (1 Samuel 1:21-25; 2:18-21,26; 3:1-9).

Eli: A Strong Case of Weak Parenting

The boy Samuel was Eli's custodial charge from the time Hannah weaned him and dedicated him to the Lord's service. This made Eli responsible for a "foster son," in addition to his primary parental responsibility of rearing his own two sons to realize their God-given potential.

Eli did a better job of rearing Samuel, it seems, than he did his own "wicked sons." Eli failed to discipline Hophni and Phinehas for corrupting the sacrificial system at Shiloh. The result of his parental laxity was catastrophic for Eli's household, but instructive for delinquent dads ever since.

By violating Jewish custom and law regarding the ritual sacrifices (1 Samuel 2:13-17,22,29), Eli's sons showed how greedy, promiscuous, and profane they were. They greedily wanted the best parts of the meat sacrifices for themselves—*more* (an extra helping), *first* (before God), *roasted* (not boiled, as prescribed by law), and *forced* (not voluntary on the part of worshipers). Furthermore, by sleeping with women in the temple, they behaved promiscuously and profanely—no better than the cultic prostitutes of Canaanite religion.

Hophni and Phinehas were guilty of profaning the ark, not only because it ended up captured by the Philistines (4:11,17,22), but because the two sons shared a pagan superstition. They identified the divine presence with the material object and incorrectly thought they could curry God's favor by manipulating the symbol as a good luck charm. For this they were killed.

Evidently, this was a case of overly permissive parenting. Eli loved his wicked *sons* but did not hate their *sins*. Hence, God disciplined Eli's sons for him by cutting off Eli's household.

Hophni and Phinehas were not the only ones who suffered the Lord's chastening in this case study. So did Eli. He stoically grieved the loss of his sons, seeing in their death both fulfillment of prophecy and evidence of his own failure to discipline. So shocked was Eli by this realization that it literally knocked him off his rocker. He was dead when his head hit the floor (4:17-18).

Caring Enough to Confront

We honor God and bring out the best in our children when we dare to discipline sinful behaviors. A father's loving and just reprimand brings life. We ought to pray for God to bless "our daily rod" as much as "our daily bread"—that we might provide the firm boundaries and loving support that our children need.

By issuing only a mild rebuke and not removing his sons from the priestly office, Eli may have thought he was putting family first or protecting family honor. We can only surmise he did not have the courage for the necessary discipline, and that saving face was his top concern. By looking the other way, Eli naively hoped the sin would go away.

Some Will Be Samuels, Others Will Rebel Like Hophni and Phinehas

Hophni, Phinehas and Samuel—all children under Eli's charge—illustrate another point: Children under our care can turn out differently from one another, even with good parental intent and teamwork. The children in whom we invest will not always respond favorably to God or bear fruit in His service. Some will be Samuels; others will rebel, like Hophni and Phinehas.

How children turn out spiritually is not capricious. It depends not only on parental input, but also on the quality of the child's relationship with God. That relationship can be helped by a parent's dedicated prayers. While the focus of this biblical case study will be on what the father Eli could and should have done, his sons obviously shoulder blame.

Caution: No guilt-tripping intended or allowed

You may be suffering the loss of your children through no fault of your own, so do not read too much into this case study, inferring guilt where none is applicable. Ask the group for an opportunity to explain your loss and seek their prayers and support. But be wary of prematurely consoling someone who pines under the Lord's chastening, lest you hinder the spiritual growth God intends.

Questions for Group Warm-up

These get-acquainted questions can be answered without reading the thematic introduction or doing the Bible study for this chapter.

1. Consider this scenario: You've warned your school-age child three times, "If you don't pick up your Lego blocks, I'll throw them out." It's two hours later and they are still on the floor. What do you do?

- ☐ Throw them away.
- ☐ Give my son one more chance.
- ☐ Pick them up myself.
- ☐ Pretend I didn't say or see anything.
- ☐ Kick myself for making a threat I didn't intend to act upon.

Now consider the same scenario, but place your foster child or stepson (if you have one) in the place of the boy who failed to pick up his Legos. Is your reaction any different? What does that tell you?

On a more sobering note, imagine that your son is about to do something dangerous, destructive, or illegal. What do you do then?

2. To help discern whether you are more authoritarian or more permissive than your dad was, consider the following table of comparative rules/expectations. Which of the following statements are true of you? (You may then pick one true-false statement to illustrate or elaborate upon for the sake of fostering group discussion.)

T F I am (or will be) more authoritarian than my dad ever was on the use of cigarettes, alcohol, and/or drugs.
T F I am (or will be) more up front on issues of age-appropriate sex-education, teen sexuality, dating, and marriage preparation.
T F I am (or will be) more consistent than my dad about household chores and consequences for not doing them.
T F I am more reluctant than my dad to spank or use physical punishment.
T F I am more conscientious than Dad in teaching God's Word regarding behaviors or attitudes incumbent upon "good" kids.

Questions for Bible Study

Read 1 Samuel 1-4 and the additional selections noted below. Then continue your group study by individually answering these questions and sharing with others from your notes.

3. What Jewish customs and laws did Hophni and Phinehas violate, (2:12-17,22,29)? For help in identifying how they were greedy, promiscuous, or profane, check the Scriptures below. (If you are doing this in a group, take one selection apiece and report your findings.)

Leviticus 4:10,26,31,35

Leviticus 7:28-36

Leviticus 10:14-15

Numbers 6:19-20

Deuteronomy 18:1-5

Deuteronomy 23:17-18

1 Kings 14:24; 15:12; 22:46

4. What effect does the death of Hophni and Phinehas have on Eli (2:31-34; 3:11-12; 4:11-18)?

Why do you suppose Eli received the prophecies and news of their death so stoically?

- ☐ Eli is more distraught and distracted by the loss of the ark than the loss of his sons.
- ☐ Eli is more upset by losing the priestly office outside his family.
- ☐ Eli realizes his own days are numbered.
- ☐ Eli realizes God is to be feared most of all.
- ☐ Other (please explain):

5. Was this tragedy inevitable (2:22-25,30,35; 3:12-13)? Why or why not?

b. If not, how could Eli have avoided this tragedy?

6. No profile of Eli as a father would be complete without a look at his foster parenting of Samuel (1:21-25; 2:18-21,26; 3:1-10,19-21). How does Eli teach God's ways in the bedtime scene with the boy Samuel?

7. Why do you suppose the Lord speaks to Samuel and not to Eli?

- ☐ Eli was deaf to the Lord answering Hannah's prayer, just as Eli could not distinguish her heart-felt prayer from drunken stupor (1:13-16).
- ☐ Old man Eli was bypassed in favor of the next generation.
- ☐ God *was* speaking to Eli, but only *indirectly*—through Samuel (also the unnamed man of God); this is God's custom with hard-of-hearing types.
- ☐ That Eli recognizes the voice as the Lord's indicates he was at least conversant with God, with a heart open to spiritual things.
- ☐ Other (please explain):

Questions for Application

This third set of questions is designed to bring the point home to yourself and other fathers.

8. Many parents fail to administer discipline because of some negative experiences. Others were waylaid by a child-rearing book that scorned all punishment as brutal, vindictive or abusive. However, godly discipline does reflect the Father God's *love* for His true children (Hebrews 12:5-11). Such discipline aims for *reconciliation* ("it will teach him a lesson"), while upholding the interests of *justice* ("he had it coming to him"). For Eli to remove his wicked sons from the priestly office would have been a just and loving act of discipline. Yet Eli ducked this responsibility as many passive dads are inclined to do. **Question:** When have you or your parents ducked a tough disciplinary issue, preferring passive neglect or, on the other extreme, harsh punishment?

9. When has a severe chastening served as a divine wake-up call, alerting you to what God wanted?

- ☐ When I received news of a sudden death in the family.
- ☐ When they terminated me from a job I held for a long time.
- ☐ When I was served notice my wife was leaving me.
- ☐ When I lost custody of my kids due to some irresponsibility on my part.
- ☐ When my rebel sons got into big trouble with the law.
- ☐ When I saw how destructive a particular sin was to my family and myself.
- ☐ Other (please explain):

10. Despite failure with Hophni and Phinehas, Eli evidently does a better job as foster parent with Samuel. From the time Samuel was first dedicated by Hannah with a Nazirite's life-long vow (1:11,17,26-28), Eli trained him to hear and heed the Lord's voice (3:8-9,17-21). How have you trained *yourself* to distinguish God's voice from competing voices?

11. When have you taken special measures to expose children under your care to the Word of God and His corrective discipline?

What could you do now, beginning this week, to make sure that they get this exposure and grow up knowing God's love through His Word?

12. **(Optional)** In relation to the children under your charge—in teaching, coaching, or parenting roles—evaluate yourself.[2] On a scale of 1 (not at all) to 5 (always), rate how you relate as a father-figure.

a. I take the lead: 1 2 3 4 5
b. I am forceful/assertive: 1 2 3 4 5
c. I make strong decisions: 1 2 3 4 5
d. I express anger at wrongs: 1 2 3 4 5
e. I set firm boundaries: 1 2 3 4 5
f. I set and enforce rules: 1 2 3 4 5
g. I tackle problems: 1 2 3 4 5
h. I resolve conflicts: 1 2 3 4 5
i. I hold people accountable: 1 2 3 4 5

Report the results of this pop quiz to your group. To get more honest feedback, ask a loved one who has seen how you parent to cross-check your answers. (Where you might put yourself in the middle, a loved one might score you at one extreme or the other.) If changes are in order, be systematic and realistic. Set small and attainable goals for more effective disciplining. Ask a trusted friend to encourage you and hold you accountable.

THE REST OF THE STORY

Hannah and Elkanah were Samuel's non-custodial birth parents. They may have felt some of the jealously and competition many parents feel when their child is being reared by someone else.

Hannah and Elkanah sent annual care packages (a homemade robe) and experienced the pangs of letting go (2:18-21). We can only speculate that Hannah and Elkanah were happy and fulfilled as parents of five other children and in their role as intercessors and visitors in Samuel's life. Hannah and Elkanah were assured by God and Eli that they had done their very best by Samuel and that he was in good hands.

They model what all parents, custodial and non-custodial, can and should do for their children: Give them to God and pray for them, as none of us know enough to rear children on our own.

The death of the well-intentioned Eli marks the end of an era in Israel's redemptive history. Before Eli, Israel was led by judges; after Eli's death, kings ruled. Samuel is a key transitional figure who set the stage for the next era, the reign of King David. Thanks to a spiritual head start from his birth mother Hannah and foster father Eli, Samuel became a prophet of the Lord and judge of Israel. It was Samuel who nominated and anointed the first two kings of Israel—Saul and David—as prophesied in Hannah's prayer (2:10). Samuel's story marks a new era in God's relationship with His people under David's kingdom, which is the main focus of 1 and 2 Samuel.

Our Next "Dad of the Week"

The story of Eli and his sons is not the only example of a delinquent dad highlighted in the Bible. As we shall see in the next two chapters, David's family exhibited incest, rape, brother killing brother, betrayal, and a parent in pain. David himself was guilty of adultery, murder, and cover-up (2 Samuel 11-12). He reaps what he sowed—his sons were but a bad chip off the old block (2 Samuel 13-18). David appears powerless to stop the violent abuse; he could only weep over his losses.

In preparation for the next session, read 2 Samuel 11-18 and reflect on what it means to be the "Wounded Father."

Endnotes

1. Documented by many sources, but adapted here from the teaching of Gary Smalley, particularly his seminar *Hidden Keys to Successful Parenting* and his books: *The Key to Your Child's Heart* (Waco, Texas: Word, 1992), chapter 2; with John Trent, *The Two Sides of Love* (Colorado Springs: Gary Smalley and John Trent, 1990, 1992), chapters 1-2, 10-12. All rights reserved, international copyright secured, used by permission of Focus on the Family.

2. Abbreviated and adapted from Gary Smalley, *The Two Sides of Love* (Colorado Springs: Focus on the Family, 1990), pp. 20-23. Used with permission.

—•••—

Who of us is mature enough for offspring before the offspring themselves arrive? The value of marriage is not that adults produce children but that children produce adults."

Peter De Vries (1910-)

—•••—

"Friction in the family, or rather lack of it, depends not so much on who you are living with as on who you are. When we submit ourselves to the hand of God that whittles away at our attitudes and behavior patterns to change and transform them, the atmosphere of our home can radically change.... Whether friction in the family becomes frightening, fragmenting or fortifying depends largely on how parents handle it."

Joyce Huggett, *Creative Conflict*

—•••—

David and Other Wounded Fathers: Feeling Helpless to Heal the Dysfunctional Past

The problem of domestic abuse against women and children is so tragic that it ought to be a topic of concern to church men's groups. Yet men seem to have difficulty even talking about it. I, for one, was shocked to find out how pervasive the problem is.

"Hitting close to home"—The problem of domestic violence

The cycle of violence and abuse within families, generation after generation, is well documented:

- At least one of every three girls, and one out of four boys, will be sexually molested before age eighteen.
- One of nine adults was a childhood victim of family sexual abuse.
- Most abuse was committed by a family member: father, mother, stepparent, uncle or sibling; but some were committed by babysitters, teachers, coaches, family friends, even ministers.[1]

Yet much violence against women and children goes unreported. Victims remain quiet to protect friends or family members who are the perpetrators; sometimes silence stems from fear of reprisals. Research studies estimate, for example, that strangers commit only 22% of reported rape. The remainder of the rapes were committed by someone the victim knew, a case we have come to call "date rape" or "acquaintance rape." Rape by whatever name is not about sex, much less about love; it is about physical and emotional abuse of power.[2]

Abuse takes other insidious forms. Children who see Dad beating up Mom, for example, learn early on to settle disputes with their fists. The rash of teenagers now being tried as adults for criminal assault, gang-related violence, and deadly force were, in all likelihood, themselves childhood victims of horrible abuse.

The "battered spouse syndrome" makes a similar point in portraying women who kill their husband-abusers as chronic abuse victims who committed justifiable homicide. Depending on what studies you read, 63 to 81 percent of abusive spouses were themselves abused as children or witnessed their parents perpetuate this cycle of violence on one another.[3]

From Gary Smalley, of Today's Family, we gain some anecdotal insight into this long-standing, intergenerational problem of abuse:

> A friend of mine grew up in a home where his father used to beat his mother. This happened right in front of him: dad pounding his fists, jerking chunks of hair right out of his mom's head. After witnessing this, my friend, just a little boy then, would run outside, screaming to get away. One time, when he was able to get away and stay at his grandma's home overnight, he could hear his grandpa beating his grandma. Then and there, at age eight, he made a decision that if he ever got married, he would never touch his wife. He knew, too well, what would happen if he did: the anger he grew up with and witnessed would spill over. Anger is like a virus we catch from our parents and grandparents, a virus that extends to the next generation and perpetuates unhealthy behavior.[4]

The growing domestic violence and recovery movement has declared a war on child and spousal abuse. Victims are now testifying before clergy groups, congressional hearings, and court rooms. Notorious cases are reported live on TV while others are replayed for our titillation and emulation in TV docudramas. "Copy-cat" versions of this violence are then often lived out in households of TV-viewers across America.

The conspiracy of silence has been broken for most victims, but the cycle of violence continues uninterrupted, as life imitates art which reflects life.

"Violence Begets Violence"—The Story of David's Family

Scripture does not shy away from reporting rape and other violent acts committed by and against other family members or trusted "friends." In David's violence-prone family, as reported in 2 Samuel 11-18 and 1 Kings 1-2, we see the makings of a script for a 1990s TV docudrama.

Don't you think the story of this ancient promise keeper would make for a riveting TV mini-series on domestic violence? Consider these scenarios: An intergenerational cycle of abuse results in rape and murder. Family honor, sibling rivalry, deception, and conspiracy are all pursued with a vengeance. The patriarch presiding over this mess says nothing and does nothing to intervene, and thus shares culpability.

I can foresee one major drawback: The cast of characters and web of relationships in this blended family is almost too dysfunctional and incredible for even modern scriptwriters to buy. Can you imagine anyone but David rising to the top of his profession while having to support eight wives, with whom he had 17 to 20 sons and daughters? Not in our society.

Just the opposite is true in most cases I know about. When one 16-year-old boy in Madison, Wisconsin, was convicted in May, 1993, for selling crack and sentenced to a ten-year jail term, it was noted in the pre-sentence report that his father had been sentenced to prison the previous month and had "fathered" *more than twenty-five children by four women.* This worst-case "deadbeat dad" used the fact of his 25 children, many of whom were familiar faces in Dane County courtrooms, as his excuse for running afoul of the law himself.

This one-man population crisis was as prolific as David and other biblical patriarchs, but that's where the resemblance stops. Such "indiscriminate fathering"—merely conceiving a child and abandoning him physically, financially and morally—is anathema to the Genesis mandate for fathers ("be fruitful and increase in number"). This man was no David, as we shall see.

David's prolific family also proliferated violence. Although eight wives and "umpteen" kids may provide a comical overtone for TV, or an excuse for running away from your responsibilities under God, David's story provides a serious look at family violence.

David is typical of many parents who know abuse or violence is occurring, but who rationalize it away as normal ("Boys will be boys"). David's life tells us that doing right is very difficult, while doing what is expedient and self-advancing is relatively easy (but cowardly). David was an angry and mournful father. He was also inattentive, fearful and absent; he exercised no control and took no moral responsibility for his own house (2 Samuel 13:21,37; also 1 Kings 1:6). David was powerless to stop the carnage of his conflicted family. He could only angrily shout and pout, or regretfully weep and reap (2 Samuel 13:21,36-37).

How tragic that fathers fail to provide the spiritual guidance or protective services necessary to break the cycle of violence under their own roof.

Amnon and Absalom grew up knowing their father had taken another man's wife for himself and then killed her husband to cover up his sin and justify his adultery. When Amnon raped his half-sister Tamar and Absalom avenged her disgrace by killing his half-brother Amnon, we have a sense of *déjà vu.* Could it be that Amnon saw in Tamar what David saw in Bathsheba—a sexual conquest with whom he could "prove" his power and masculinity? Was this another case of "like father, like son"?

Tamar protested Amnon's advances to no avail.[5] He ignored, overpowered, and raped her. Then, in frustration and anger, he somehow fancied that Tamar was the provocative one—the scapegoat who must now be banished.

Men who rape do not know the real target of their anger. Angry men like Amnon regard women as objects for ego-gratification and scapegoats for blame-shifting. Sometimes, their real problem is a dysfunctional childhood, for which they are justifiably angry at their parents or society in general. But "justifiable anger never justifies abuse."[6]

The Self-Inflicted Wounds of a Do-Nothing Father

Though "furious" and grieved at what he heard, David proved to be a passive, do-nothing dad in relation to both the son who rapes and the son who murders. Perhaps David did nothing to punish either son because of a misguided father's love ("he can do no wrong"), or perhaps fear of public opinion (he was king, after all). Most likely David felt compromised, hypocritical and powerless ("How can I punish my son for sexual sin or murder or lying when I was once guilty of the same?").

If this retaliatory domestic violence took place in today's understand-all-but-punish-nothing culture, a sympathetic case could be made by Absalom's legal and psychological defense team: Because David did nothing to punish Amnon or reconcile his hurting family, Absalom had no choice but to root out the evil, take matters into his own hands, and kill Amnon.

Had David exercised the discipline of expulsion, this would have been a credit to his parenting skill, assertiveness, and moral backbone. Instead, King David "mourned for his son every day" and later "kissed Absalom" when he returned.

This act of kissing and making up bypassed any repentance or justice. Without reconciliation, this reunion bore bad fruit. Absalom undermined and usurped his father's kingdom by using David's parental laxity to convince David's subjects that their king would act unjustly (2 Samuel 15:2-6). True repentance and justice might have broken the cycle of family violence.

Just as Eli failed to remove his two morally derelict sons from priestly office, so David backed down when discipline was needed. Perhaps David hesitated to discipline Absalom out of fear of public opinion, or guilt and hypocrisy. In Absalom, he could see not only a handsome charismatic figure in his own likeness, but also a replay and amplification of his own sinful past. No doubt a penitent David tortured himself with the realization that the calamity ripping his family down the middle began with his sin against Bathsheba and Uriah.

The focus of this week's study is the emotional wounds and spiritual abuse (neglect) either suffered by or perpetrated by David himself, who stood idly by instead of stepping in.

Questions for Group Warm-up

These get-acquainted questions can be answered without reading the thematic introduction or doing the Bible study for this chapter.

1. Which of the following was true of your dating experiences as a teenager?

- ☐ I imagined "falling in love" with any girl who "made eyes" at me.
- ☐ I went to great lengths to "accidentally" cross her path and strike up a conversation.
- ☐ It was "puppy love," not the real thing.
- ☐ I was frequently goaded into "scoring" with women inappropriately.
- ☐ I was manipulative and insecure in needing to "have" a girl.
- ☐ If my feelings ever took on a perverse twist, I checked out what to do with someone I trusted.
- ☐ I was a late bloomer and did not notice girls back then.
- ☐ Other (please explain):

2. Did you ever become "lovesick" for a girl you could not have? (Perhaps someone else's girl, a girl from another culture, religion or social class; a cousin, or some other relative?) What was that like?

Questions for Bible Study

Read 2 Samuel 13:1-15:14; skim chapters 11-12; 16:15-23; 18:1-33. Then continue your group study by individually answering these questions and sharing with others from your notes.

3. What advice does Amnon receive to help him seduce Tamar (13:1- 11)?

b. Does this scheming power play "work," or does it backfire (13:12-19)? How so?

4. To what extent is David an unwitting party to both the rape scheme and its aftermath (13:6-7,13,21)?

5. Suppose it was Tamar's word against Amnon's in modern jury trial.

a. Would Tamar make a credible witness for the prosecution against Amnon? (What evidence could she bring forward? What damages could she sue for?)

b. How would Tamar fair under cross-examination by Amnon's legal and psychological defense team? (What "evidence" or "testimony" might be used against her to get Amnon off the hook?)

6. Empathize with David in this crisis situation, which would test the competency of the most effective father. Why doesn't he do what any ruling judge and self-respecting father would do in this crisis?

7. Even though "justifiable anger never justifies abuse," we can still empathize with Absalom. Why do you suppose he did what he did?

- ☐ Blood ties are thicker than anything else that binds (or breaks) a blended family.
- ☐ Even before this incident, Absalom wanted a pretense to bump off Amnon to be next in line to succeed David on the throne.
- ☐ There's no telling what Absalom was up to, since he advised Tamar to forgive and forget, while he himself hated Amnon (13:20,22).
- ☐ Amnon was killed in the heat of the moment, under the influence of alcohol.
- ☐ If David had punished Amnon, Absalom wouldn't have had to.
- ☐ Men are entitled, even obligated, to retaliate for violence done to a family member.
- ☐ Jacob's sons avenged the shame brought on their sister Dinah, so why can't Absalom avenge his sister Tamar?
- ☐ Other (please explain):

Questions for Application

This third set of questions is designed to bring the point home to yourself and other fathers.

8. In what ways have your self-esteem, marriage and/or parenting style been affected by past sexual sins (yours or someone else's)?

- ☐ Not being a virgin when first married was held against me.
- ☐ I regret premarital sex that hindered bonding to my wife.
- ☐ I had trouble trusting or bonding in an intimate relationship.
- ☐ I feel compromised in my ability to discipline; now I must tell my kids, "Don't do as I did, do as I say."

- ☐ I have nurtured bitterness, anger, and/or guilt from my childhood that now targets other innocent people.
- ☐ I know the forgiveness of God and can offer that to others.
- ☐ Without knowing it, I married "damaged goods" and I want my money back.
- ☐ Even though I escaped a dysfunctional past or a previous marriage with relatively little collateral damage, my kids have not.
- ☐ Other (please explain):

9. Whether Absalom fled for his own good, or David expelled him for doing wrong, this incident raises an interesting case in point for other parents of rebellious youths. Under what circumstances, if ever, would you expel a problem child in your family?

b. Under what conditions would you take back that child?

10. Are you afraid of becoming like your father—or that your kids will become like you? How so?

11. Perhaps you, or some in your study group, have failed to exercise the disciplinary measures needed to restore the family honor and break the cycle of violence. Wrestle with the question: *Why does God allow sin to be reproduced within the family?* (Is that fair? How do we escape?) Listen to fellow victims and perpetrators describe their pain and sorrow. Don't judge one another. Resist the temptation to shift blame (as in, "She made me do it," or "My parents were that way to me").

12. Review Psalm 51 in light of 2 Samuel 11-13. Reflect on how God used traumatic events in David's family to produce a penitential psalm. David's remorse in Psalm 51 touches people who suffer similar pain and wonder what to do with their emotions (of denial, bargaining, anger, grief, and acceptance). As a broken man, David was more usable by God. *Can you identify with the emotions of David poured out in Psalm 51? How so?* Pray about what comes up in your group, or in pairs, as you have time.

The Rest of the Story

David's affair with Bathsheba sounds like a mid-life crisis. Such a crisis happens to many men (also women) over 40. Life has become routine or boring, and battle scars on the work and home fronts may have taken their toll on a fragile ego. In either event, David's sin not only destroyed the existing family of Bathsheba and Uriah, but took its toll on the rest of his blended family. The new family of David and Bathsheba was also destroyed; the child of their adultery died soon after birth.

While David's sexual sins and moral laxity contributed to his family's pain, he recovered his relationship with God through repentance and forgiveness. All his life David was a "man after God's own heart" (1 Samuel 13:14; Acts 13:22). Absalom, by contrast, was not so inclined to God. He sinned over and over in his attempts to steal the hearts of the people (2 Samuel 15:1-6). The revolt of Absalom was due to bad blood, bad fruit, and bad parenting in this badly blended family. Not that his revolt was inevitable or excusable. The man who lives by the sword will die by the sword. Absalom's rebellion against his father came to a violent but just end (15:1-14; 16:21-22), as did the insurrection organized by another sibling, Adonijah (1 Kings 1-2). Both deaths by the sword fulfilled Nathan's prophecy that David's clan would be plagued by violence (2 Samuel 12:10-12).

It was a younger sibling, Solomon, who received his father's blessing and became the royal successor. Solomon's great, elder-like wisdom was forged in the trials growing up in David's family. But that is the subject of another chapter (see Chapter 7).

Our Next "Dad of the Week"

Before we get to Solomon, we will consider another installment of David's parenting experiences. Part II of David's story is more positive: We see him as a foster parent who takes in a fatherless, disabled youth, Mephibosheth. David does so out of loyalty to Jonathan's family. Boys who grow up without their fathers and without full use of their limbs or other faculties, as did Mephibosheth, are twice handicapped. Physically and emotionally impaired children pose considerable challenges to any parent who takes custody of them.

In preparation for this next chapter on fathering, read 1 Samuel 20:14-17; 2 Samuel 4:4; 9:1-13; 16:1-4; 19:24-30; 21:7-9. Then reflect again on what it means for "David and other Nurturing Fathers" to provide father love and foster care for those growing up without fathers.

Endnotes

1. These statistics are generally accepted by most experts in the mental health profession and protective services. These particular figures are quoted by Cecil Murphey in his guidebook, *Mantalk: Resources for Exploring Male Issues* (Presbyterian Publishing House, Louisville, KY: 1991), in which he cited a booklet by Euan Bear, with Peter T. Dimock, *Adults Molested as Children* (New York State Council of Churches: 1988).

2. Report of the Wisconsin Coalition Against Sexual Assault (1992).

3. The case has been made by research consultants on family violence—Richard Gelles, Nancy Jurik, Coramae Mann, Jan Stets, Murray Straus, Kersti Yllo, among others—that domestic abuse is mutual. Contrary to popular belief and the "politically correct" position, husbands and wives are abusing one another in roughly equal numbers (24 percent of domestic violence cases is initiated by women, 27 percent by men, and the rest is mutual or inconclusive).

Recent research stipulates, however, a few caveats for interpreting the accumulating evidence: the injuries inflicted by women are not as damaging as those by men; men don't live in chronic fear of abusive wives, as do battered women of their abusive husbands, boy friends or ex-lovers; many (but not most) women who are violent do so as an act of self-defense or retaliation; and if sexual assault cases (date rape, etc.) were factored into the studies of physical assaults, the incidence of male-initiated violence would be higher. Not factored into most of these research studies is the rising incidence of "false memory syndrome," which is just coming to light.

4. Excerpt from Gary Smalley, *Homes of Honor Relationship Series* (Today's Family, Branson, MO: 1994), page 52. Used with permission.

5. Also, Tamar's marriage proposal (2 Samuel 13:13) is a diversionary tactic, meant to buy time and elude Amnon's immediate designs. Such a marriage between siblings of a common father was prohibited by Hebrew law (Leviticus 18:9; 20:17; Deuteronomy 27:22). Adding insult to injury, the prospect of marriage to someone else was now tainted, as Tamar was no longer a virgin. Tamar's protest stands in contrast to Bathsheba's willingness. Bathsheba sounded no protest to David's invitation for a tryst; one could say "she asked for it" by cleaning up and perfuming herself before coming over (11:2-4).

6. So says Madison-based therapist, Darald Hanusa, Ph.D.

—•••—

It would be a blessing if each human being were stricken blind and deaf for a few days at some time during his adult life. Darkness would make him more appreciative of sight; silence would teach him the joys of sound."
Helen Adams Keller (1880-1968)

—•••—

"The most handicapped (person) in the world is a negative thinker."
Heather Whitestone, Miss America 1994

—•••—

"Our Father yet heals the spirit of amputees—even when they will not grow legs. And, once the spirit is healed, the legs can be done without."
Calvin Miller

—•••—

CHAPTER SIX, PART II

David and Other Nurturing Fathers: Fulfilling Covenants and "Father Hunger" for "Special Needs" and Foster Kids

Ever since the TV sitcom, *Murphy Brown*, mocked the importance of fathers and Vice President Dan Quayle publicly begged to differ, several noted sociologists, educators, and political pundits have jumped on the bandwagon. They ask "Where have all the fathers gone?"

With twenty-five to forty percent of American kids now growing up without their fathers in the home,[1] more and more are left to wonder: *Mommy, where do daddies come from?* Mounting evidence is exposing the ugly social and emotional consequences of children growing up without fathers. Kids from fatherless homes show academic underachievement, higher truancy, more unruly behaviors, and increased juvenile delinquency. Boys who lack a strong father presence in the home go through life always trying to prove their masculinity—chasing women, picking fights, or getting every raise and promotion they can.[2]

The Hunger of the Fatherless Mephibosheth

If he were alive today, Jonathan's sole surviving son, Mephibosheth (a.k.a. Merib-Baal, 1 Chronicles 8:34), could stand up and speak to this issue of *father hunger*. That is, if he could even "stand up." Orphaned at the tender age of five when Saul and Jonathan died fighting Philistine armies (1 Samuel 31; 2 Samuel 1), and crippled in both feet from a childhood accident (2 Samuel 4:4; 9:13), Mephibosheth *knew* father hunger.

But Mephibosheth suffered even more than the loss of two father figures and two limbs; he was also "emotionally impaired." He grew up in a home where he saw fits of jealous rage, murder attempts, loyalty conflicts, cruel deceptions and denials of reality—what therapists call "crazy-making." The besieged household of his manic-depressive grandfather, King Saul, was a frightening home for a small child.

As loyal a friend as Jonathan was to David ("he loved him as himself," 1 Samuel 18:1,3), we can only surmise that Jonathan must have been a very loving and nurturing mentor to his own son. That's what makes Mephibosheth's orphan status even more pitiable. Without a father's love, and feeling dropped (literally) by his primary care-givers, Mephibosheth had reason to feel like "a dead dog" (2 Samuel 9:8), abandoned and undeserving of a king's attention when David comes calling.

You know that David was Israel's finest warrior-king and a "man after God's own heart" (1 Samuel 13:14; Acts 13:22). But did you know that David was also a foster father of an orphan? And that he parented a handicapped boy, in addition to his umpteen other sons?

The Promise of a Foster Father

That's right. King David took in the young prince Mephibosheth some years after the death of his parents. To get Mephibosheth, now a young adult with a son, Mica, David went well out of his way, clear across the country.[3] Mephibosheth and Mica were mooching off Makir, a wealthy godfather or benefactor (2 Samuel 9:4). The situation seems like that of an unwed teenager or welfare dependent. The man had no "independent living" skills and was living with anyone who could meet his "special needs." No doubt he hungered for a father to fill the void left by the death of Jonathan.

Out of covenant loyalty to Jonathan (1 Samuel 20:14-17; 24:21), David protected and provided for this orphan prince at great risk and expense to himself. Kings in David's position normally killed off all surviving rival claimants to the throne—which is what Mephibosheth was. David did not. He was a nurturing father and a man of his word.

I wonder how many nurturing fathers there are today who have "Jonathan and David" loyalty toward each other? How many covenant to make "your child mine?"

A Composite Profile of the "Good Father"

My interest in this subject of father love and foster care was piqued by the results of a nationwide survey conducted by *Redbook* magazine and printed in its June '93 issue. The survey dealt with fathers *responsibilities* and *behavior* ("What makes a *good* father?"), not just personal rights or the political rhetoric. I like that! To learn how fathering may have evolved from the way we were reared, the survey also noted intergenerational comparisons, not just father-mother comparisons. I shall pursue that comparison further in the rest of this chapter.

I suspect that many divorced fathers, like me, were less involved in hands-on parenting when married the first time. With no one to share (or delegate) those parental duties, I became more involved. When divorced dads bring this experience in hands-on parenting and nurturing to a second marriage, they are more pro-active in co-parenting. Still, mothers and others want to know if members of the fathers' rights movement still fight for, or even bother with, the *mundane* aspects of fathering. That is, will they feed, diaper, dress, or stay home with a sick or disabled child?

He may be a good man, but "Does he do diapers?"

Why is a man's commitment to childcare equated with his willingness to change diapers or miss a day of work when the child is sick? I'm not sure, but this question ("Does he do diapers?") was put to me by a family court counselor inquiring about my hands-on fathering.[4]

Unlike their dads, half the respondents in *Redbook*'s survey ventured out alone—without their wives—to buy children's clothes. An astonishing 86 percent have apparently made solo trips to the pediatrician. Three quarters of today's dads knew their child's favorite toy, current weight, or favorite food or teacher. This generation of dads is also noted for reading books on parenting. (I'll say "Amen!"—for that means more readers for this book.)

Nurturing: the human instinct

Judging from these and other survey questions, today's dads consistently outperform the previous generation in the nurturing department. The Christian men's movement is part of a larger trend that is beginning to overturn the long-held, cultural belief that women are more nurturing, caring, compassionate, and committed to service. That may be an old myth, but kids all know, by social conditioning, which parent to cry for after falling down.

(That's right: "M-o-o-o-mmm-e-e-e!")

The myth that nurturing or care-giving is natural to women and foreign to men has worked to a woman's *dis*advantage too. Women have shouldered the vast majority of caretaking and nurturing tasks. This demanding responsibility has been expected of women because of this nurturing myth. But this instinct is not wired only into a woman's nature; nurturing is possible and common to *human* nature.

Double-income families and those with a female bread-winner and a full-time dad, are both discovering this truth. (Did you hear the latest twist, the one about the couple who wanted the Mommy track and the Daddy track at work? They each called a nanny to go and take care of their careers, while both husband and wife stayed home to pursue their kids!)

As men are relieved of the pressure to work all the time, or if they are on their own as single parents, they will discover their God-given potential to be nurturing. I made this discovery as a single parent nine years ago. Before then, my first wife lay claim to the ability and duties of childcare. I first confronted this cultural and gender stereotype when I was seen pushing strollers years ago. Several passersby thought

I was "babysitting" or "*helping* Mom with the kids." That makes me wonder what cultural and gender stereotypes David ran into when he cared for Mephibosheth? ("Hey, this isn't king's work." "Warriors don't belong in the home." "Foster care is not for fathers.")

Where are all the (foster) fathers?

On this last point, the Dane County Department of Human Services, where I've received my training in foster care, regrettably agrees that too few fathers are in foster care. Of 400+ homes currently licensed in Dane County, in only one home is the primary licensee a father.

King David did not stay home and provide all the foster care or nurturing needs of Mephibosheth by himself. Nonetheless, David and Mephibosheth regularly enjoyed mealtimes together, as did the king with his other sons. David saw to it that all of Mephibosheth's special needs were met: "All the members of Ziba's household were servants of Mephibosheth" (2 Samuel 9:10-12).

Contrary to popular opinion, longitudinal studies have shown that when fathers do stay home by choice, the children universally thrive. Even when the stay-at-home parenting option is forced by career dead-ends or because their wives made more money, their children still thrived under dad's care.[5]

Our biblical story illustrates that the converse is also true. Mephibosheth suffered great emotional wounds when deprived of his real father at such an early age. His need for unconditional love from a significant male adult may have been at the root of Mephibosheth's statement of self-pity, "What is your servant, that you should notice a dead dog like me?" (2 Samuel 9:8).[6]

Lesson from David's life for other nurturing fathers

David was a going-out-of-my-way foster father. His story counters the prevailing social trend in America that says "fatherhood is a voluntary commitment." Many Davids now provide father love and foster care for a Mephibosheth they know.

David pledged himself to be a foster father who made a difference. As a "man after God's own heart," he reflected God's love in his covenant of "steadfast kindness" toward Jonathan's family. Because David received father-love from God and brother-love from Jonathan, he could love Jonathan's son in like manner.

That same divine and transferable father love is available to us if we will be men after God's own heart, consciously passing that father-love on to our own children or someone else's.

No doubt the "physically challenged" and "emotionally impaired" Mephibosheth was a difficult and demanding person to love and care for. But as my mother-in-law says, "When your kids are the most unlovable, that's when they need loving the most." God honors promise-keeping dads like David, who keep their word at all costs.

Questions for Group Warm-up

These get-acquainted questions can be answered without reading the thematic introduction or doing the Bible study for this chapter.

1. Have you or your own children suffered any serious or lingering illness, injury, or disability? (What kind? For how long?)

In each case, how did that affect family relationships, especially between father and child? (Were you willing to fully support them, especially when the giving on your part seemed mostly one way?)

2. Who would you name in your will to care for your minor children in the event something should happen to you and your spouse?

Conversely, are you named to assume parental duties for anyone?

Questions for Bible Study

Read 1 Samuel 20:14-17; 2 Samuel 4:4; 9:1-13; 16:1-4; 19:24- 30; 21:7-9. Then continue your group study by individually answering these questions and sharing with others from your notes.

3. How did Mephibosheth lose two fathers and two limbs?

4. Do you think Mephibosheth was disabled or impaired in any way other than his obvious physical lameness? Why or why not?

5. What made David's entry into the world of foster care different than most dads today?

6. What factors do you suppose David weighed in making this big foster care decision?

- ☐ The town of Lo Debar (2 Samuel 9:4) is deep in Gilead territory far from Saul's family estate and David's court.

- ☐ The lameness of Mephibosheth meant extra servants would have to be hired to meet his special needs.
- ☐ The son of Mephibosheth meant double-duty, like caring for one of today's unwed teenagers.
- ☐ Saul's considerable estate, which Mephibosheth alone had inherited, would cover the cost of child care.
- ☐ David was primarily motivated by his promise to Jonathan.
- ☐ For David, as for others in foster care, fatherhood is a voluntary commitment, and he freely volunteered to do it.
- ☐ David might have considered how an attention-getting person with special needs would impact the rest of his family.
- ☐ David took him in sight unseen, so becoming a foster parent was a "no-brainer" for him.

7. Suppose you were David weighing the uncorroborated evidence and conflicting testimony of Ziba (2 Samuel 16:1-4) and Mephibosheth (19:24-30).

a. Regarding Mephibosheth's true reason for staying back in Jerusalem, who do you think is telling the truth and why?

b. First David gave Mephibosheth's rightful inheritance to Ziba (16:4) as the chief steward of that estate. After giving to Ziba all of Saul's estate that rightfully belonged to Mephibosheth, David then decided to withhold judgment and split the difference, with half of Saul's estate going to Ziba and half to Mephibosheth (19:29). Was David being prudent, lazy, tricked again, one-sided, double-minded, fair, waffling, or what?

c. What would you have done (differently) as Mephibosheth's foster father to discern the truth and/or address the indebtedness to Ziba? (What do you do when you hear conflicting testimony from your kids: Split the difference? get to the bottom of it? give in to guilt? or what?)

Questions for Application

This third set of questions is designed to bring the point home to yourself and other fathers.

8. Noted sociologists, educators, and political pundits have been asking: "Where have all the fathers gone?" The fatherless inner-city boy asks, "Mommy, where do daddies come from?" *How would you answer them?*

- ☐ Our culture has made dads optional or expendable, as personified in the TV sitcom *Murphy Brown* and the divorce courts that strip men of their kids.
- ☐ Anthropologist Margaret Mead said it best: "Fathers are a biological necessity but a social accident."
- ☐ Men view fathering as volunteer work, a burdensome chore.
- ☐ Men lack role models of what is a real father; they can't give to others what they never received themselves.
- ☐ Fatherlessness isn't the problem; lack or loss of father love is.
- ☐ Other (please explain):

9. Do you know any modern-day Mephibosheths?

- ☐ Orphans (from war, AIDS, gang violence):
- ☐ The "physically challenged":
- ☐ The "emotionally impaired" (suffering from loss of father love):
- ☐ Those in need of foster care:
- ☐ Other (please explain):

10. From all the Mephibosheths you know, what kinds of disabilities—physical, emotional or relational—would you find it hardest to live with or care for?

11. Imagine you're presented with the need and opportunity to provide father-love and foster care to such a Mephibosheth today. Would you do it? Why or why not? What is your opinion of father-love and foster care?

- ☐ It's too demanding.
- ☐ I let someone else raise the kids.
- ☐ "Father hunger" overwhelms me.
- ☐ I need a "Daddy track" at work.
- ☐ I can say to another promise keeper, with Jonathan-David loyalty, "Your child is mine."
- ☐ All this talk is just so much psychobabble.
- ☐ I'm doing just fine, thanks for asking.
- ☐ Other (please explain):

12. It's not only orphans or disabled youth who feel like "a dead dog." Many others miss their fathers. What has contributed to your sense of father hunger?

- ☐ My dad was very distant emotionally, never really there for me.
- ☐ Due to pain and confusion in our home, I withdrew.
- ☐ My parents divorced, dad left; the home I knew was gone.
- ☐ I lost my dad early on due to ill health and subsequent death.
- ☐ My dad was a "no-show"—physically, financially, morally.
- ☐ My parents couldn't handle me and often sent me away.
- ☐ Other (please explain):

The Rest of the Story

Though treated royally and given the honor of eating at David's table all his life, Mephibosheth is later alleged to have betrayed David. He may have schemed to take back his kingdom (2 Samuel 16:3).[7] David was unsure whom or what to believe, but remained faithful to Mephibosheth. One more time David spared his foster son's life. Were it not for David's intervention, the Gibeonites' murderous purge of Saul's household would have included his foster son, too (21:7-9).[8]

While David was powerless to break the intergenerational cycle of violence and sexual immorality within his own household (see Part I of David's story, pages 66-68), he is to be commended for succeeding with Mephibosheth, whose life he enhanced and spared. David's story as a father brings us, one generation later, to Solomon and his "seven hundred wives of royal birth and three hundred concubines" (1 Kings 11:3).

Our Next "Dad of the Week"

Solomon knew the trials and tribulations of growing up in David's mixed-up brood. He ruled wisely and justly for forty years on David's throne, but toward the end, the bane of blended families (1000 foreign wives!) got to him. The record of that achievement and downfall, plus the wisdom learned thereby, is preserved for us principally in three books: 1 Kings 1-11, Ecclesiastes, and Proverbs. That's the story we take up in Chapter 7, "Solomon and the 'Wise Elder' Tradition."

In preparation for this next chapter on fathering, read 1 Kings 1:28-3:28; 4:29-34; 5:3-5; 8:10-21; 9:1-9; and 11:1-13. Then reflect on what it means to be a "Wise Elder," able to speak proverbial wisdom learned from the School of Hard Knocks.

Endnotes

1. Figures vary depending on what studies you read, but some generally accepted findings, summarized in *Parents* magazine (July 1993), are these: Nearly 25% of children born in this country today live in female-headed households. More than half of all American children can expect to live in such households before they turn eighteen. Of the kids living in female-headed households, only 12% spend even one night a month in their father's home, while 40% have not even seen their fathers for a year or more.

2. See Frank Pittman, *Man Enough: Fathers, Sons and the Search for Masculinity* (G. P. Putnam's Sons, New York: 1993).

3. The town of Lo Debar (2 Samuel 9:4) is deep in Gilead territory, well across the Jordan, far from Saul's family estate and David's court.

4. When this question was posed to the dads in the *Redbook* 1993 survey, it should surprise no one that 96 percent of the respondents said yes. But what surprised me is that 40 percent said that their dads never did change any diapers! Likewise, 80 percent of today's dads were involved at regular times in the feeding of their young ones, compared to only one third of their dads.

5. These are the findings of Kyle Pruett, M.D., renown psychiatrist at Yale University and author of *The Nurturing Father* (Warner Books, NYC: 1987). He conducted longitudinal studies, spanning a decade, of eighteen families where the man stayed home to raise the children.

6. Admittedly, one can only guess at the emotional pain experienced by Mephibosheth at the loss of father love. Perhaps he grew up always feeling left behind or abandoned—like "a dead dog." Or perhaps that particular metaphor expresses only how Mephibosheth felt in the unexpected presence of the king.

7. It could well be that Mephibosheth had nothing to do with Ziba's allegation. Perhaps he was framed by his servant instead, and Mephibosheth's "lame excuse" was sincere (19:26), which is what his unkempt appearance (19:24) is meant to convey. Or it could be that they were both hedging their bets on the outcome of Absalom's rebellion and wanted to be in the best possible position to accede to the throne if David should die.

8. The "Mephibosheth" they killed among Saul's descendants (2 Samuel 21:8) was Saul's son by his concubine Rizpah, not to be confused with the son of Jonathan. The latter produced a long line of descendants for Saul (1 Chronicles 8:34-38).

—•••—

When one generation is on the verge of denying the ability of God to do something, bring in the elders! They have the knowledge, history, and experience with God to know what really happened, how God works, and how you should trust Him today. The goal is to be a gray-headed old man with some wisdom to pass on to the next generation."

Robert Hicks, *The Masculine Journey*

—•••—

"Don't expect wisdom to come into your life like great chunks of rock on a conveyor belt. It isn't like that. It's not splashy and bold,. . .nor is it dispensed like a prescription across a counter. Wisdom comes privately from God as a byproduct of right decisions, godly reactions, and the application of spiritual principles to daily circumstances. Wisdom comes. . .not from trying to do great things for God. . .but more from being faithful to the small, obscure tasks few people ever see."

Charles R. Swindoll (1934-)

—•••—

CHAPTER SEVEN

Solomon and the "Wise Elder" Tradition: Giving and Heeding Father-Son Advice

At age twenty-five I was ordained a *ruling elder* in my church and a year later a *teaching elder* in my denomination. Since becoming more involved in the men's movement through the Promise Keepers, I have come to understand "elder" in a new light, as not necessarily a church board member or clergyperson.

I now see an *elder* as someone further along the road spiritually and experientially than someone only in his or her twenties. An elder is someone who can disciple me in the faith as a growing child of God, who can mentor me in my work as a free- lance Christian writer, and who can coach me in my role as a growing husband and father. I know few men who have filled one or another aspect of that tall order.

The credibility of any father's or elder's wisdom rests on his ability to "walk the talk." By this criteria, King Solomon was allegedly the wisest man of his era (1 Kings 4:30-31). Yet he made a number of compromises and eventually his heart grew cold to God (1 Kings 11:1-6). This bundle of contradictions presents an interesting case study, but before we get into it, I invite you to reflect along with me on the elders (father figures, wise men or mentors) who have made a real difference in our lives.

Elders who made a difference

The elders I have known and appreciated were qualified not so much by age or church office, as by inner character, servanthood, and spiritual endowment. Each of these men demonstrated a fatherly interest and a willingness to pour his life into someone else.

My first mentor was "Coach K," a High School football coach in the Vince Lombardi tradition ("When the going gets tough, the tough get going"). While he had little to do with my coming to faith four years later, he had everything to do with growing certain character qualities and leadership abilities in me. I earned the team's MVP award for captaining an undefeated, unscored-upon defense in my senior year.

But I almost didn't make it to my senior year. I had been given the ignominious award, "Hell Driver of the Year," by the outgoing senior class, and for good reason. I was hell-bent on destroying myself by taking too many chances behind the wheel. That's when Coach K gave me a sobering, life-saving talk about living up to my responsibilities as football captain. That's all it took to straighten me up to fly right. That talk and one other mentor: John.

John was an *elder* in traditional senses of the word, as he pastored a church in my hometown of Pleasantville, New York. Although I never attended his church during my turbulent high school years, John and his wife Muriel were my second parents. They took me under their wing and coached me through various spiritual, marital, and career decisions. That mentoring process resulted in my eventually coming to faith in Jesus Christ during college, in my decision to marry for the first time at age 23 (counter to John's counsel), and in my accepting a call to serve Christ on college campuses with InterVarsity Christian Fellowship in the 1970s.

My third spiritual father was Bruce. He took me under his wing as an apprentice staff worker with IVCF. He modeled a love for Christian books and *biblical* teaching and application to life that is my vocation today. Bruce and his wife reintroduced me to the Holy Spirit and the ways of God, much as Priscilla and Aquila did for the young evangelist Apollos (Acts 18:24-28). Bruce also introduced me to racquetball, the one sport I've played continuously and competitively since grad school. I am now discipling my boys into this combination of faith and sports.

After my apprentice years under Bruce, other elders showed a fatherly interest in my ministry of the Word—first with InterVarsity, then with Serendipity, and now with the "Gruen Group." I owe a debt of gratitude to Pete, "Dr. A," Lyman, Dick, and Ray, among others in this wise elder tradition.

Where is Solomon when we need him?

But I'd trade all of them in for one wise elder to help me mature on the husband and father front. Would that I had a Solomon in my life today! I'd like an elder to confront me head-to-head when I go astray. I need an elder to protect my back when I'm under attack. The right elder would harness himself shoulder-to-shoulder with me when my parenting load is too heavy. A particularly wise elder might whisper proverbial wisdom in my ear when I'm questioning what to do. A Solomon in my life might help me settle sibling rivalry disputes, peaceably resolve custody disputes with my ex-wife, and make ethical choices in my everyday work.

Solomon was a "peculiarly rich mentor."[1] He was rich in wealth, but more so in choices. That makes Solomon a particularly apt mentor for us who have so many choices (such as what job to accept, where to live, which lifestyle to adopt). We may not have his unique reputation for international trade and imported riches (1 Kings 10), nor his largess for public works projects and palatial homes (1 Kings 5-7).

Though not rich in any of these traditional respects, we do have a wealth of *choices* or options—more than we know what to do with—which makes us "rich" and Solomonic by definition.

We can also identify with Solomon the fallen sinner, often discouraged and led astray by others. But God still used him. When God gives wisdom—as a spiritual gift—it is not dependent on our human ingenuity or educational degrees. When God bears fruit, He can do it in spite of or because of us.

Do we want wisdom? Do we want to be wise leaders, fathers, mentors like Solomon? Then ask. "If any of you lacks wisdom, he should ask God, who gives generously to all without finding fault, . . .but when he asks, he must believe and not doubt (James 1:5-6).

Venerable wisdom for fathers comes from living through traumas or passages in parenting—whether that be coping with childlessness, parenting teenagers, or mentoring the extended family. Younger fathers lack that wisdom of experience. "Tool Time" Tim Allen, on the TV sitcom *Home Improvement,* is always receiving this wisdom of experience from his across-the-fence neighbor, Mr. Wilson. I'd regularly consult a neighbor like that, too. What Solomon and others in the "wise elder" tradition have in abundance is this wisdom of hindsight.

Understanding the Enigma of Solomon

Solomon was the tenth son of David and second with Bathsheba. He was a replacement child for the one they conceived and lost as a consequence of their adulterous and murderous love affair. Solomon grew up in a most confusing family structure (with eight moms and 16-19 siblings). His childhood was rife with horrible violence, including non-stop family feuds, one brother raping his half-sister and two other brothers killing their half-brothers. (See Chapter 6, Part I of David's story.)

Solomon grew up with a decorated war hero for a father, and with a war widow and ambitious power-behind-the-throne woman for a mom. Countering their intentions for Solomon were his vengeful and murderous siblings. This marked Solomon as a man of destiny. Bathsheba, the most ambitious of David's eight wives, lobbied for her son's right to David's throne even as his father and her husband lay dying (1 Kings 1-2).

Solomon, whose name means "peaceable," grew weary of war and yearned for peace, that he might build the temple his warrior father never could (1 Kings 5:3-5). In spite of his sin, David's faith in God ran deep and unbroken. Solomon's faith was shallow and compromising (1 Kings 3:3) and his heart grew cold toward God late in life, because "he did not follow the Lord completely" (11:1-6). Solomon's lust for women was untempered and unparalleled; his 1000 wives and concubines make his father (with *only* eight wives) look like an innocent choir boy.

With an appetite for more of everything than anyone else, Solomon became Israel's most ambitious king. This product of royal privilege and a dysfunctional family developed considerable skills at dispute resolution, successful living, government, building operations, international relations, and cultural achievement (1 Kings 3-10; 2 Chronicles 1-9). His outward success hid, or perhaps compensated for, his soul's misery.

Despite all his women, wealth and fame—or maybe because of them—Solomon became cynical. He found his life, in the end, devoid of any joy or significance. Wrestling with his troubled soul and unmet aspirations, Solomon exhausted "everything under the sun" and came up empty (see Book of Ecclesiastes). His life and legacy of hedonism reveals the bankruptcy of a life full of self instead of dependence on God.

The Book of Ecclesiastes, a compilation of Solomon's more cynical wisdom, is a study in the kingdom of Self, not the kingdom of God. A quick read-through of Ecclesiastes shows that perhaps Solomon learned from his mistakes and wanted his sons not to repeat them. From his failures and pain, and with the wisdom of hindsight, he concludes, "Remember your Creator in the days of your youth. . . . Fear God and keep his commandments, for this is the whole duty of man. For God will bring every deed into judgment, including every hidden thing, whether it is good or evil" (Ecclesiastes 12:1,13,14).

Solomon wearied of studying books (12:12), yet he was prodigious in this department, too. He had a way with words, such that he spoke 3000 proverbs and 1005 songs (1 Kings 4:32), and was known to collect many more, only a portion of which are found in holy Scripture. Our study of Solomon will consider a few of these proverbs for insight from a "wise elder" who has been there before us and learned the hard way.

Questions for Group Warm-up

These get-acquainted questions can be answered without reading the thematic introduction or doing the Bible study for this chapter.

1. In your younger years, who took a fatherly interest in or began a mentoring relationship with you? (Jot names here, for future reference.)

a. Specifically, in your scholastic achievement or job performance?

b. Specifically, in your home life, as a husband or father?

c. Specifically, in your Christian life, as a disciple of Jesus Christ?

2. What favorite saying of your father's was applied to a variety of situations and sticks with you to this day? (The saying could be something proverbial, notorious, seemingly trivial, or said for laughs. You may also draw upon any memorable sayings you grew up with, even if uttered by a father figure other than your dad.)

Questions for Bible Study

Read 1 Kings 1:28-3:28; 4:29-34; 5:3-5; 8:10-21; 9:1-9; and 11:1-13. Then continue your group study by individually answering these questions and sharing with others from your notes.

3. Why would Solomon want wisdom above all else (1 Kings 3:1-15)?

- ☐ To succeed in marriage, especially with all those foreign wives.
- ☐ To parent wisely because raising the children conceived by 1000 wives and concubines is no small task.
- ☐ To rule justly in all political and judicial questions put to him.
- ☐ To make up for the fact that he was only half the man of God that David was.
- ☐ With wisdom comes prosperity, the real goal.
- ☐ Solomon's modesty kept him from asking God for more.
- ☐ Solomon didn't trust God to give him anything but wisdom.
- ☐ Other (please explain):

4. What issues, insights, feelings, and ethical dilemmas were involved in Solomon settling a parent's worst nightmare—a death of a child and losing a custody fight (1 Kings 3:16-28)?

What parenting dilemma (sibling rivalry, custody fight, or property dispute) of yours has required Solomonic wisdom to distinguish between two or more plausible alternatives?

5. Solomon committed considerable resources (human, financial and natural) to build the temple to honor God's name (1 Kings 5-7). In what sense, and under what conditions, is God present in this temple (1 Kings 8:10-21; 9:1-9)?

6. David's dying wish was for Solomon to "be strong, show yourself to be a man" (1 Kings 2:2). No doubt that saying echoed in Solomon's head and heart the rest of his life. What do you suppose the saying, "be a man," really meant to Solomon?

☐ The *Ladies' Man* (with 700 wives, 300 concubines).
☐ The *Mafioso* (strong, stoic, surrounded by hired guns like Benaiah).
☐ The *Self-Made Man* (building monuments to Self).
☐ The *Marlboro Man* (lover of horses and wide open country).
☐ The *Wise Man* (author of Proverbs, philosopher of life).
☐ The *Warrior Man* (a decorated military hero like David).
☐ The *Sensitive Man* (author of emotive psalms, as was David).
☐ The *Godly Man* ("a man after God's own heart," a promise keeper).
☐ Other (please identify):

Suppose your father's dying wish to you was like David's to Solomon: "Be a man." What understanding of manhood did your father live out or symbolize for you, as typified by his favorite sayings or life message?

Likewise, what would it mean for you and your sons if you were to tell them with your life message: "Be a man?"

7. Solomon went on to formulate and collect proverbial sayings that conveyed what spiritual maturity ("being a man") looked like in practical ways. Look up each of these proverbs, if you have time; otherwise divide them up among your group and report back to one another. What does each set of proverbs say about the *role of a father in helping a son become a man?* About the *role of an elder in helping a young man mature?*

a. *Sex education* begins in the home, following the example of Dad: Proverbs 2:1,16; 5:1-5; 15-23; 6:20-35; 7:1-27.

b. *Financial education* is also Dad's duty:
Proverbs 3:1-2,9-10,27-28; 6:1-5; 11:1-6; 16:1-3,9.

c. Teaching your child the *value of hard work* is another parental duty: Proverbs 6:6-11; 10:4-5; 12:11,24; 13:4,18,22; 14:4,23-24; 16:26; 19:15; 20:13; 21:17,25.

d. Fathers should maintain both *discipline and grace* in the home: Proverbs 3:3-6,11-12; 4:1-9; 13:24; 19:18; 22:15; 29:15,17.

8. Why do you think a preponderance of his proverbs deal with these father-son themes of sex, money, hard work, and success?

- ☐ Solomon had his own problems with women, riches, and fame.
- ☐ Solomon's kids had problems in these areas.
- ☐ Solomon had God's insight into the deceitful human heart.
- ☐ Solomon had future generations in mind when he composed and collected this wisdom teaching.
- ☐ As a hedonist, despairing of meaning and spiritually apostate, Solomon was an unworthy example as a mentor to anyone.
- ☐ I would need Solomon's wisdom to figure this one out!

9. How do you account for Solomon's heart growing cold toward God (1 Kings 11:1-6)?

- ☐ He was like the temple edifice—great for show and tell, but only a shell until the Lord fills it with His presence.
- ☐ He violated the terms of the covenant God spelled out ("If you walk before me in integrity of heart.... But if you or your sons turn away...." *See also* Deuteronomy 17:14-17).
- ☐ He gave his foreign wives freedom to practice their pagan religion under his roof; such cultural diversity proved to be his undoing.
- ☐ He didn't take to heart his own preaching, but kept it only in his head.
- ☐ Keenly aware of sinful human nature, he could learn from others' mistakes but needed a mentor to help him with his own.
- ☐ Power, like wine, intoxicates even the best of hearts; no man is wise enough to be trusted with unlimited amounts of power.
- ☐ Other (please explain):

Questions for Application

This third set of questions is designed to bring the point home to yourself and other fathers.

10. Suppose you had an extra dose of Solomonic wisdom available right now. In what particular problem area do you, a family member, or someone you are mentoring, need that wisdom?

11. If you wanted the kind of wisdom given to Solomon, how would you go about getting it? (See the Chuck Swindoll quote, page 84.)

- ☐ Dream on! (God speaks to me through my dreams.)
- ☐ By practical obedience to the commands of God already given.
- ☐ By reading Proverbs each day and the whole Bible in one year.
- ☐ By reading "wisdom books" recommended by my mentor—legal, history, self-help, biography, murder mystery, or whatever.
- ☐ By faithfully making the right everyday decisions and successfully doing the little things that go unnoticed.
- ☐ By making more mistakes in life, asking for feedback, and receiving correction from my clients, family, peers, and elders.
- ☐ By holding myself accountable to another person or group.
- ☐ By asking God for an anointing of the spiritual gift of wisdom.
- ☐ Other (please explain):

12. When we come to recognize our mistakes, we have wisdom to pass along, even if it is of the "Do as I say, not as I did" variety. In this regard, what wisdom in hindsight do you have for a son about being a man, or for another man about becoming mature?

The Rest of the Story

Lover, financial planner, builder, power broker, international statesman, writer, poet, judge, CEO, military leader, worship leader—Solomon was all of that and more. Conspicuously absent from the biblical accounts of Solomon (1 Kings 1-11; 2 Chronicles 1-9; Proverbs; Ecclesiastes; Song of Solomon) is any mention of his role as husband or father. Yet we know that he had at least one son, named Rehoboam by his wife Naamah the Ammonite (1 Kings 14:21,31). Rehoboam succeeded to Solomon's throne at age 41 (11:43). Whether Solomon was a mentoring father who made much of a difference in son Rehoboam, Scripture is mostly silent.

However, one incident in the life of the adult Rehoboam is most revealing as to whether he learned to heed the wise counsel of elders.

As a new king, Rehoboam did not heed the counsel of wise elders who urged him to extend tax relief to the general populace. The people were overburdened by taxation to support Solomon's expansive, budget-busting government. Instead, he listened to younger men who had not lived through Solomon's harsh years. Their arrogant and foolish advice was to rule by harshness, not kindness. This gross miscalculation, spurning the advice of wise elders, led to a rebellion against Rehoboam led by the ten northern tribes. The tribes split off from Israel and divided the monarchy by naming Jeroboam their king (1 Kings 12).

Thus, by good and bad examples in the family and kingdom of Solomon, we learn the value of hearing and heeding wise father- son advice. Godly advice can make a difference in how we raise our families, lead other people, or govern the nation.

Our Next "Dad of the Week"

The story of Solomon and the wise elder tradition brings us, in short order, to Elijah and Elisha, two prophets who enjoyed a father-son type mentoring relationship. Together they illustrate the value of establishing a spiritual mentoring relationship that will, in the Lord's timing, "turn the hearts of the fathers to their children, and the hearts of children to their fathers" (Malachi 4:6).

In preparation for this next chapter on fathering, read 1 Kings 17-19 and 2 Kings 2:1—8:6; then reflect on what it means to be a "Father Who Mentors."

Endnotes

1. One of my mentors, InterVarsity's Pete Hammond, brought me onto the *Word In Life Study Bible* project team as a contributing writer of biblical personality profiles. For many of the insights into Solomon as mentor cited here, I am indebted to an article Pete wrote for *The Word In Life Study Bible*, (c) 1995 by Thomas Nelson, Inc. Used by permission.

—•••—

men•tor [from the Greek *Mentor*]: **1** *cap* a friend of Odysseus entrusted with the education of Odysseus' son Telemachus; **2a:** a trusted counselor or guide; **b:** TUTOR COACH.
Webster's Ninth (1983-)

—•••—

"[Mentoring is] the phenomenon where people just starting out need three things to succeed: a dream (goal, ambition, vision, plan); someone who believes in them and can help bring their dream to reality; and determination. Mentors are then helpers who are there, but not necessarily the ensurers of success."
Robert Hicks, *The Masculine Journey,*
quoting The Uncommon Individual Foundation

—•••—

"Fathering is the highest form of mentoring."
David DeWitt, *The Mature Man: Becoming a Man of Impact*

—•••—

CHAPTER EIGHT

Elijah and Other "Fathers" who Mentor: Passing the Mantle of Leadership to Others

Use your sanctified imagination. Suppose you were the Lord's advance man wielding a magic sword imbued with "the spirit and power of Elijah." Imagine that by waving it in certain directions, you could reconcile fathers and their children. Think about what you could eliminate: No more back talk or generation gap. . . . No more communication breakdowns or personality clashes with an "ex". . . . No more broken homes or un-blended stepfamilies.

Imagine, furthermore, that your spiritually-endowed, Elijah-patented sword could not only eliminate obstacles to father-child reconciliation, but also replace all that brokenness with close-knit intimacy. Imagine yourself enjoying glorious father-son tournaments. . . harmonious father-daughter talks. . . gregarious family reunions.

Dream on!

And get real. If you have been estranged from your children or your parents for any period of time, Elijah bids you to examine your heart of hearts. Whatever it takes to soften a hardened heart and turn toward home and family—meditate on that.

With that powerful wand in hand, which set of relationships would you change: A rebellious son? An estranged daughter? Aloof stepchildren? A languishing relationship with your own father or stepfather? Lonely kids in neighborhood street gangs?

The force of Elijah bonds fathers and their children

You may be amused by this vision of a powerful force, as if it were something from *Back to the Future* or *Star Wars.* Such a dreamy scenario may look and feel impossible. But God is not bound by our human limitations. Actually, the scenario I've imagined here is not unlike the voice of one crying in the wilderness—specifically, the voice of an Elijah.

> See, I will send you the prophet Elijah before that great and dreadful day of the LORD comes. He will turn the hearts of the fathers to their children, and the hearts of the children to their fathers; or else I will come and strike the land with a curse (Malachi 4:5-6).
> And he [John the Baptist] will go on before the Lord in the spirit and power of Elijah, to turn the hearts of fathers to their children and the disobedient to the wisdom of the righteous, to make ready a people prepared for the Lord (Luke 1:17).

According to Malachi and Luke, on the day of the Lord the hearts of fathers and their children return to each other. True reconciliation is accomplished. The mighty sword of Elijah truly saves the day.

Yet such reconciliation will not take place in a *single* 24-hour day. It has taken generations, even millennia, but "that great and dreadful day" (of the Lord's coming) will fully restore the father-child bond, never to be broken again. Perhaps you doubt this will ever come to pass this side of heaven—"especially not on my side of the family," you say. That may be so. But I pray "our Father who art in heaven" will hasten the day of its coming for us fathers who *aren't* in heaven and live emotionally or physically apart from our kids. . .and our dads.

The day "Father" Elijah was ushered into heaven

The day "Father" Elijah was ushered into heaven provides us with a glimpse of the mentoring relationship Elisha enjoyed with him. Their relationship is a model for us as we are mentored and as we find children or students to mentor in turn. I've seen it happen—but (usually) without deep waters parting or chariots of fire ascending. For those special effects, you'll have to envision those two prophets on Elijah's way to heaven (2 Kings 2:1-12).[1]

Forewarned by other prophets about Elijah's imminent departure, Elisha aggressively stayed at his master's side: "As surely as the Lord lives and as you live, I will never leave you," he said (2:2,4,6). As the two walked from Gilgal to Bethel to Jericho to the River Jordan and beyond, Elisha was beside his master every step of the way.

In today's parlance, we'd say that Elisha was *in his face*; that's how closely he pursued Elijah. Elisha stuck around long enough and close enough to get what he wanted, which was a double portion of Elijah's spirit (2:9-10). Elisha realized that discipleship is better "caught" than "taught," and he certainly caught the mantel of leadership (and more!) from Elijah (2:13-15).

A mentor couldn't ask for a better protégé or replacement than Elisha. A successor couldn't ask for a better example to follow than Elijah. Elisha not only learned from his master all that he could in a short span, he stood on his master's spiritual shoulders in his own ministry to the poor and the powerful. The senior miracle-worker must have been proud of all his junior partner accomplished in his absence. (For a comparison of the two, see chart on page 103.)

Elijah was a classic mentor in several respects. He was primed for the job by a wounding experience which left him depressed, even suicidal: "I have had enough, Lord," he said. "Take my life; I am no better than my ancestors" (1 Kings 19:4). Elijah tried to take a well-deserved retirement after defeating the 450 prophets of Baal and fleeing from the murderous Queen Jezebel. But the Lord would not allow him to quit. First he had to anoint and train Elisha as his successor (19:16-21). God renewed his spirit, and Elijah was obedient to the task of mentoring his protégé.

The Elijah-Elisha model tells us that mentoring relationships must be God-ordained and student-driven. Yet successful mentoring entails three steps on the part of the mentor:

(1) imparting a vision (Martin Luther King: "I have a dream");

(2) helping that dream become a reality (the Promise Keeper's motto: "back to back, shoulder to shoulder"); and;

(3) modeling success and expecting great things from the successor ("I did, and so can you").

No mentor can ensure that success, however, as so much depends on the protégé's initiative and follow-through. A successful mentoring relationship also has God as the third party enabling and ensuring success by His Spirit, even a "double portion" of it, as in Elisha's case. God's spiritual endowment and Elisha's personal discipline enabled him to do far more than his master, much as the students we mentor or children we raise will exceed us.

Fathering is like mentoring. Mentoring is like discipling. Father-like mentoring can be secular or Christian in focus. In academia, athletics, the creative arts, and business, secular mentors are the norm. When the veteran Barnabas mentored the convert Saul, who later mentored young Timothy, we see mentoring as Christian discipleship (see Chapter 12).

The parallel between fathering and mentoring may be deduced from E. Paul Torrance's well-researched book, *Mentor Relationships: How They Aid Creative Achievement, Endure, Change, and Die.* Here's what researchers have learned that pertains both to the fathering and the mentoring tradition of Elijah and Elisha:[2]

(1) Mentoring does make a difference; 84% of mentored people say they adopted at least some characteristics of their mentor.

(2) Protégés feel "positive" (87%), even "very positive" (73%) about their mentors.

(3) All mentoring relationships come to end sometime, but in 52% of the cases the interpersonal relationships were sustained long-term (at least for the twenty-two-year stretch of this particular study).

(4) Where mentoring relationships proved temporary or unsustainable, several reasons were cited:

(a) The power of the mentor over his student became overbearing or abusive.
(b) The pace of the mentoring was out of sync with the student's needs (either too fast or too slow).
(c) A perceived lack of moral integrity in the mentor.
(d) The student felt boxed in by the specialization or too-narrow focus of the mentor.
(e) Bad cross-gender chemistry or relationship differences.

(5) Where mentoring relationships survived long-term or proved very positive, several reasons were cited:

(a) Students were encouraged to become passionate in their pursuit of excellence.
(b) Students were urged to go with their strengths and not waste time trying to round out their learning.
(c) Students followed their own dreams, free of the expectations of others.
(d) Students were directed to find their own master teacher and attach themselves.

By substituting "fathering" for "mentoring" in the above research findings, we see many possible applications for both family life and ministry. Let's examine a few of those.

Questions for Group Warm-up

These get-acquainted questions can be answered without reading the thematic introduction or doing the Bible study for this chapter.

1. Recall the teachers, coaches, elders, and father-figures (other than your dad) who significantly shaped your life. What made that mentoring relationship significant for you?

2. Recall your experiences teaching, coaching, counseling, or fathering. (Perhaps it was in Little League, Sunday school, as a summer camp counselor, a tutor, or professional mentor.)

a. What or who initiated that relationship?

b. What led to the relationship's success or demise (however enduring or temporary)?

QUESTIONS FOR BIBLE STUDY

Read 1 Kings 19 and 2 Kings 1:1-2:18. Then continue your group study by individually answering these questions and sharing with others from your notes.

3. How does God prepare Elijah for his role as a spiritual father or mentor to someone else (1 Kings 19)?

- ☐ Coming off a mountaintop spiritual high (defeating 450 prophets of Baal), running out of gas, and hiding in a cave (to escape Jezebel's murderous threat), lonely Elijah was ready to turn in his prophet's badge.
- ☐ Elijah was in no position to pass on the mantel of leadership as long as he was throwing a pity party for himself ("I am the only one left").
- ☐ God's therapy or rehabilitation program involved exhausting Elijah of all his excuses and resources, then rejuvenating him and recommissioning him to mentor someone else.
- ☐ Prophets don't retire; if they are obedient, they first find a replacement.
- ☐ Of all the 7000 potential candidates reserved by God, Elijah would not have known which prophet to mentor had God not named Elisha.
- ☐ Other (please explain):

4. As far as we know, Elijah had no children, yet Elisha called to him "My Father! My Father!" (2 Kings 2:12). In what sense was Elijah a father?

- ☐ In the Roman Catholic sense, he was a celibate priest.
- ☐ Their age gap required a respectful form of address.
- ☐ He idolized Elijah and confused him with the first person of the Trinity.
- ☐ Elijah was an authoritative witness to official doctrine and practice, much as the early Church Fathers.
- ☐ Elijah founded or originated a certain school of prophets and is thus regarded as the "father" of prophecy.
- ☐ Elijah and Elisha had more than a teacher-student relationship; they were more like father-son.

5. Consider the question God twice put to Elijah: "What are you doing here?" (1 Kings 19:9,13). How does Elijah answer?

6. How does Elijah establish his prophetic authority, such that both Hebrew kings (and any protégé watching) take note (2 Kings 1)?

7. After his prophetic authority is established by deeds and character reputation, how does Elijah begin mentoring Elisha more directly (2:1-10)?

8. Why do you suppose Elisha asked for a *double portion* of Elijah's spirit?

- ☐ "Double" was the firstborn son's inherited right (Deuteronomy 21:17), and Elisha was the spiritual firstborn son of his "father."
- ☐ Elisha felt inadequate to the task of succeeding Elijah and needed all the divine help he could get.
- ☐ Elisha was greedy and wanted a ministry reputation twice that of Elijah.
- ☐ I don't know have a clue.
- ☐ Other (please explain):

Questions for Application

This third set of questions is designed to bring the point home to yourself and other fathers.

9. Recall a time and place when you, too, were down and out. Perhaps you were discouraged, faced career conflict, or marital-family difficulties. Imagine that a mentor asked you the same riveting (or rallying) question that was put to Elijah, "*What* are you doing here?" ("What are *you* doing here?" "What are you doing *here*?") Your answer:

10. There comes a time in every man's life when he begins to think about *generativity*, that is, generating his vision or agenda or values in the lives of others. These treasures are passed on to up-and-coming employees, new church recruits, or family members, for example. Have you come to that place in your fathering where you are concerned about *generativity*?

How will you know if you are ready to generate your vision or agenda or values in the lives of others?

11. If you were to become known as "father" to some youngster outside your immediate family, would any of your biological children become jealous?

Conversely, have you let your children know they have (or can have) more men than you as a father-figure? (Or would you be jealous and not want another man to have that kind of influence on your child?)[3]

12. Which end of the Elijah-Elisha relationship are you currently on, and with whom? (Name them in the space provided.)

☐ I'm more the mentor, pouring my life into someone younger:

☐ I'm more the student, taken under someone else's wing:

Which end of that mentoring relationship would you like to be on during this coming year? and with whom?

(optional) What specific need do you have that you would like met in a mentoring relationship with a "father"? (Or, what "double portion" do you want?)

The Rest of the Story

Remember the playground taunt, "Anything you can do, I can do better?" Or the one, "My dad can beat your dad" at whatever contest? I see some of that comparison going on in the biblical records of Elijah (875-848 B.C.) and Elisha (848-797 B.C.). Yes, it seems, the narrators were into keeping and breaking records. Compare the chart of miracles (on page 103):

By comparing their miracles, it seems that Elisha "outperformed" Elijah—but that only means that Elisha had the better teacher!

The story of Elijah and Elisha is far from the only mentor-protégé relationship in Scripture. In fact, we shall study the Barnabas-Paul-Timothy mentoring relationship (Chapter 12), as well as Jesus' mentoring relationship with His disciples (Chapter 13).

Our Next "Dad of the Week"

Before we get to those mentoring relationships, we shall look at another non-traditional father, Mordecai. He cared for a fatherless cousin, Esther, whom he raised as his adopted daughter. Mordecai coached her to do her best as an attractive woman, a ruling matriarch, and as a liberator in the redemptive history of God's people.

In preparation for this next chapter on fathering, read the Book of Esther; then reflect on what it means to be an adoptive father who prepares other children to win at life.

Endnotes

1. Much of the insight on the Elijah-Elisha mentoring model parallel what Robert Hicks and I summarized in *The Masculine Journey Study Guide* (NavPress, Colorado Springs: 1993), pages 65-67, 76-77. Used with permission.

2. David DeWitt, in his book, *The Mature Man: Becoming a Man of Impact* (Vision House Publishing, Gresham, Oregon: 1994, pages 165-167), distills Torrance's research for our discussion of mentoring and fathering. For the complete findings, see E. Paul Torrance, *Mentor Relationships: How They Aid Creative Achievement, Endure, Change, and Die* (Bearly Unlimited, Buffalo, New York: 1984, pages 1-31).

3. I readily acknowledge a set of "second parents," John and Muriel, who mentored me during my turbulent high school and college years. They were instrumental in my eventually coming to faith and going into full-time Christian ministry (see Chapter 6, page 105). I suspect this extra set of parents was a relief for Mom and Dad, but I also know from my own stepparenting experiences how humbling it can be to take a back seat to a preferred parent.

How miracles of Elijah and Elisha compare

Elijah's miracles	Elisha's miracles
Food is brought by ravens and multiplied for widow. (1 Kings 17:5-6,12-16)	Oil is multiplied for widow; food is multiplied for prophet. (2 Kings 4:1-7, 4:42-44)
Poor widow's son is raised from the dead. (1 Kings 17:17-24)	Rich woman's son is raised from the dead. (2 Kings 4:18-27; also 8:1-6)
Altar and animals are totally consumed by fire. (1 Kings 18:16-46)	n/a
Predicts the death of King Ahaziah. (2 Kings 1:6,16-17)	Predicts the death of King Ben-Hadad (2 Kings 8:7-15)
Invokes fire to kill soldiers who would muzzle prophet. (2 Kings 1:9-14)	Invokes bear to kill youth who mock prophet's authority. (2 Kings 2:23-25)
Able to part the Jordan River and cross over on dry land. (2 Kings 2:6-8)	Able to part the Jordan River and cross over on dry land. (2 Kings 2:13-14)
Translated to heaven without dying. (2 Kings 2:11-12; compare Genesis 5:21-24 [Enoch])	Died from an illness, but his bones had the power to raise another man buried with him. (2 Kings 13:20-21)
n/a	Polluted spring is purified. (2 Kings 2:19-22)
n/a	Poison stew is purified. (2 Kings 4:38-41)
n/a	Naaman's leprosy is healed in River Jordan. (2 Kings 5:1-14)
n/a	Gehazy is made leprous. (2 Kings 5:15-27)
n/a	Iron ax head is made to float on water. (2 Kings 6:1-7)
n/a	Aramean army is turned away with blindness, while God opens the eyes of others to see God's army. (2 Kings 6:8-23)
n/a	Predicts the end of famine in besieged Samaria. (2 Kings 6:24-7:20)

"Often I am surprised when I hear people say about an adopted child, 'That poor girl. No wonder she has such a hard time. Her mother rejected her.' Or hear an adopted child say, 'I will always wonder why my mother rejected me. It's ruined my whole life.'"... Adopted children need to be taught that for most birth mothers giving up a baby is not an act of rejection. It is the most selfless, courageous, brave deed they can do. It is laying aside their own desires and longings, to bestow on that baby something greater and better than they can provide. For almost all birth mothers, a piece of themselves dies in that surrender.... They understand that without both a father and mother...the child might not be able to become all God intended him to be. Never have I met a birth mother who thoughtlessly gave her baby away."

Ann Kiemel Anderson, *Open Adoption*

CHAPTER NINE

Mordecai and Other Adoptive Fathers: Preparing Other Children to Win at Life

Our "dad of the week" is Mordecai, the adoptive father of orphaned Esther (Esther 2:7,15,20). This father and others like him are to be celebrated for how well they prepare adopted kids to become winners at life. This Mordecai study lifts up issues some adoptive fathers will face such as: adopting children under difficult circumstances; raising daughters to be winners in a man's world; giving daughters away in marriage; "letting go;" coaching daughters to seize the moment and advance God's cause.

Religious news editor:

"Mordecai and Esther, how could you?!"

Esther could write the book, *What My Dad Did Right in Raising a Winner.* I could see it published by some liberal religious news editor as a crossover book and companion volume to the Book of Esther. However, I suspect the two-volume set would be banned in some conservative religious circles for its pagan improprieties, R-rated violence, its mention of mass murder and hanging, and its failure to mention God even once. Finally, this biblical narrative is filled with scandalous implications.

I say "scandalous implications" because the story of Mordecai and Esther is fraught with faith-shattering questions and far-reaching precedents. For openers:

- How could he allow a good Jewish girl to enter into holy matrimony to a divorced pagan of another race?
- How could he marry her off to an abusive, drunken male supremacist renown for oppressing women and Jews?

King Xerxes was an angry, brutish man. His shameful divorce from Queen Vashti diminishes the luster and chance for success in a second-time-around marriage to Esther. Who of us would give our daughters in marriage to such a man? Yet God seems to sanction this risky, oil-and-water arrangement. This story underscores our belief that God uses human instruments, even pagans and mixed marriages, to accomplish His just and redemptive purposes.

However, I'm getting ahead of our story. Back to the original premise . . . that Mordecai did many things right in adopting and raising his daughter to be a winner.

ESTHER:

"I love Mordecai for what he did right in raising me."

Mordecai did right by Esther. Mosaic Law made no provision for adoption, yet he took Esther as his own child. Even Greek and Roman law provided only for adoptions of boys and citizens of the realm. Esther was neither.

In actual practice, adoptions were done: (1) if the adoptive father was childless and had no other way to perpetuate his family; (2) if the adoptive father was moved by a "deep affection," special loyalty, or kinship ties; (3) unspecified religious reasons; and (4) if the adopted son swore to abide by the legal obligations and religious affiliation of the adoptive parent.[1] The exceptional adoption of Esther by Mordecai likely fell under condition No. 2. The two were cousins (Esther 2:7), and the ties of blood and loyal affection are central to the subsequent narrative.

Mordecai not only went out of his way to adopt Esther, he went overboard to give her The Blessing.[2] Orphaned at a young age, Esther would not have had the benefit of an older man's wisdom, guidance, or affirmation. Mordecai believed in her, attached high value to her, and instilled in her an indestructible pride in her ethnic roots. She kept her Jewish identity a secret (2:10,20) not out of timidity or shame, but out of obedience (7:1-6; 8:1).

All along, in his parenting, plotting and blessing of Esther, Mordecai pictured a special future for her as the Queen of Persia who would one day liberate the Jews. Mordecai made an active commitment to fulfill that blessing, as evidenced by the behind-the-scenes arrangements he made on her behalf.

Evidently, there was no way to hide Esther's attractive qualities from the king's talent scouts. She stood out and was taken into the harem. The selection process was by king's edict and totally out of their hands. Yet Esther, following the precedent of Daniel in Babylon (Daniel 1), may have had a choice in whether to resist the king's beauty treatments and special foods. Unlike Daniel, Esther accepted without question what was prescribed for her, even if that violated Jewish custom.

Mordecai could not have planned ahead or foreseen long-term exactly how propitious the selection of Esther was. But he did want her as wise, gracious, and attractive as she could be, so that she'd be in a position to make the best of a bad situation. Later on he would want Esther to do something winsome and heroic as Queen of Persia to liberate the Jews. But for now, as God would have it, it was amazing enough that she won the national beauty contest and the king's hand in marriage.

Even if Mordecai did not plan for Esther's rise in status, he raised her right. His good fathering brought her up to fear God, to be obedient, wise and gracious. When the world of politics and diplomacy tested those virtues, she proved a winner.

Somewhere along the way, she learned that proper deference, perfect timing, and national fasting (4:1-17) were the way to gain an audience and alliance with the king (5:1-7; 7:1-3).

Esther is the heroine of the book that bears her name. The Jewish celebration of Purim that she instituted (Esther 9) is a national festival still practiced by Jews today. But that feast was originally called "Mordecai's Day."[3] This recognition of Mordecai's active role, as *the* behind-the-scenes human instrument of the Jew's deliverance, is duly noted in the punch line to the book (10:2-3).

Haman:

"I hate Mordecai and the people he represents!"

While Mordecai did right by his daughter and her husband the king, he could do no right in the eyes of Haman, "the enemy of the Jews" (8:1; 9:10,24). In a courageous stand for Jewish solidarity, Mordecai repeatedly refused to bow down and pay homage to the Persian prime minister. That sustained act of defiance earned him a spot on Haman's hate list, a list which extended to all Jews (3:1-6).

Haman the Agagite (3:1) likely descended from Agag, king of Amalek (1 Samuel 15:20), while Mordecai, a Benjamite Jew (2:5), obviously descended from Saul and Moses. Successive clans of Amalek and Moses had been battling since the days of Joshua (Exodus 17:8-16) and Saul (1 Samuel 14:47-48). So the hatred between the people of Haman and the people of Mordecai went back several centuries before these two men clashed in Susa.

Haman's plot to kill Mordecai and annihilate the Jews (3:1-15) was foiled when Queen Esther exposed Haman to the king (7:3-6). Thanks to encouragement from Mordecai (4:4-14), and the three days of fasting and prayer by other people (4:15-17), Esther was persuaded to risk initiating a meeting with the king. In a bit of "gallows humor," Scripture records that the king had Haman hanged on the same 75-foot-tall gallows Haman had prepared for Mordecai (5:14; 7:9-10). King Xerxes then made Mordecai the prime minister of Persia in Haman's stead (8:2; 9:3-4; 10:2-3).

As prime minister, Mordecai had opportunity to uproot evil and make his world a better place. He seized the moment. With all the authority invested in him, he decisively reversed Haman's fatal decree (8:7-14) and did good for the Jews (10:3). The very act of celebrating the Jews' deliverance gave many non-Jews reason to convert (8:15-17).

Mordecai:

"Learn from me how to raise a winner"

Centuries before Mordecai, Amalekites had attacked the Jews as they fled Egypt. Like wolves, they "cut off all who were lagging behind" (Deuteronomy 25:17-19). The Amalekites' cruelty and bloodlust set in motion this ethnic hatred.

Generations later, God told Saul to annihilate all the Amalekites, down to the animals in their flocks. Saul did not do so, but spared the king and choice livestock (1 Samuel 15:2-3). Saul's disobedience left the seed of an Amalekite nation. Subsequently, Mordecai and the Jews of his era were in exile and on the brink of extinction—if Haman would be allowed to carry out his plan.

The story of Esther and Mordecai shows that sin is not only personal, but incorporated deep into family histories and public policy. Such institutionalized sin is present today. Conscientious fathers will want to break this cycle in their children's lives. Haman (7:1-10) was like a token Washington bureaucrat left to "twist in the wind," for problems that are embedded in the whole fabric of administration policy and power. Getting rid of an immoral politician may appease the voters' wrath momentarily, but it is still necessary to undo the bad public policy left in place (8:7-14).

To keep such deep-rooted sin and racial hatred from extending to our children and their children, we fathers must do more than vote for clean government or keep our racial attitudes in check. We must also work to root out evil and repeal bad law. Otherwise, our children will reap the results of the evil that previous generations have sown.

The story of Mordecai encourages us to believe that good-faith efforts and righteousness will not always go unrewarded by God. In God's economy, "what goes around comes around." God oversees the plot twists and "chance coincidences" in our lives, as He did in the Mordecai-Haman turnabout. He does this to uproot sin and accomplish His just and redemptive purposes through us.

Good News:

"God overturns our sour grapes theology"

Believing "what goes around comes around" has a double edge. What I call "sour grapes" theology, some call victimology. Both have dangerous, unbiblical corollaries. An ancient piece of proverbial wisdom was: "The fathers have eaten sour grapes, and the children's teeth are on edge" (Jeremiah 31:29; Ezekiel 18:2). Which is to say, that whatever the fathers had done (eat bad grapes), the subsequent generations were now experiencing (gnashing of teeth, or sour taste in the mouth).

Can't you hear the "sour grapes" talking among those caught up in the *victimization* syndrome? Listen to them gnash their teeth, saying (about their suffering in exile): "It's not our fault. We don't deserve this punishment. It was our parents' fault. We're not responsible."

At one level I agree with this thinking. Jerusalem was destroyed in 586 B.C. and its people exiled largely because God was "punishing the children for the sins of their fathers to the third and fourth generation" (Exodus 20:5). Likewise today, children from dysfunctional families *are* victimized by "bad parents," who, in turn, are only parenting the way they were parented.

But at another level, a gut level, I disavow victimology or sour grapes theology.

We are not merely helpless victims and virtual orphans of bad parenting. The sins of our fathers, no matter how cruel or grievous, do not trap us into some "life sentence" cycle of crime and punishment. Passing the buck up the line to our forefathers ultimately engulfs us in self-pity, fatalism and despair.[4]

We are all responsible agents. We can repent of our sinful past, break the cycle, and help shape a more hopeful future. This applies even to victims of the cycle of poverty, government welfare, and ghetto crime. Loving counsel says, "Yes, at one level you are the victim of bad parenting. You have suffered from the sins of others. But blaming others does not absolve you or resolve your situation. Only God's all-sufficient grace can do that."

Furthermore, I agree with Mordecai that we must be pro-active (as instruments of God's grace) to break the cycle, undo the damage, and restore the well-being of our families. We can adopt orphaned children, as he did, and thus help one child at a time. But we can also follow the example of Mordecai in taking a public stand for faith, believing God "for such a time as this" (Esther 4:14). God can use us in our present life-positions to make something good of our lives, to do good to others, and to repeal bad laws affecting the well-being of our children and their children.

Let's take a closer look at how God used Mordecai to do just that.

Questions for Group Warm-up

These get-acquainted questions can be answered without reading the thematic introduction or doing the Bible study for this chapter.

1. Do you know anyone who has given up their child for adoption?

What was it like for the birth parents to let go, and what were the mitigating circumstances? (In this regard, reread the opening quote from Ann Kiemel Anderson, page 104.)

2. Do you know anyone who has adopted a child?

What was it like for the adoptive parents to take on someone new? (To what lengths did they go? Was the adoption complicated by race? by delays? by second thoughts? by siblings' reactions?)

Questions for Bible Study

Read the Book of Esther. Its compelling drama and ironic plot twists make Esther a quick read. Then continue your group study by individually answering the following questions based on that book and reporting your findings to the group.

3. Our opening questions were not rhetorical. Try answering one:

a. How could he allow a good Jewish girl to enter into holy matrimony to a divorced pagan of another race?

b. How could he marry off her to an abusive, drunken male supremacist renown for oppressing women and Jews?

- ☐ Mordecai was an opportunist who schemed to get himself into public office on his daughter's petticoat.
- ☐ Mordecai and Esther were like Pollyanna—naive about sin and evil.
- ☐ They did not think bad things could happen to good people.
- ☐ Mordecai must have surrendered his daughter to God for such an unlikely scenario to ever have a chance of succeeding.
- ☐ God willed "such a time as this," so I can't second guess it.
- ☐ This story is so secular that any talk of "God's will" is a scandal.
- ☐ It appears Mordecai had no such misgivings about giving away his adopted daughter in this marriage.
- ☐ I believe that nothing—not even mismatched marriages—happen to God's people by accident, chance, or human conspiracy.
- ☐ I haven't a clue.

4. King Xerxes fares poorly in most retellings of the Mordecai-Esther story. Yet I see hope in this narrative for second marriages. What evidence do you see that his second wife, Esther, made Xerxes a better husband and ruler than he was when married to Queen Vashti? (Or was he the same all the way through, a husband no wife could change for the better?)

5. Consider how difficult it must have been for Esther to keep secrets from her husband (2:10,20) and to remain loyal to Mordecai (2:11,22; 4:4-17), especially when life-and-death issues were at stake. What insight does this give you into the tension between husband-wife and father-daughter relationships?

6. What do you suppose Mordecai was doing just outside the king's gate (2:21; 4:2; 5:13)?

- ☐ Idling the time away, eavesdropping on conversations.
- ☐ Cooking up conspiracy theories for an Oliver Stone movie based on Esther.

- ☐ Working in some official capacity, minding his own business.
- ☐ Having trouble "letting go" and trusting the king with his daughter.
- ☐ Pouting and protesting until he got his way.
- ☐ Other (please explain):

7. Consider the long-standing enmity between the people of Haman and people of Mordecai (3:1-6). What insight does that give you into the nature of sin and its institutional forms, such as racist public policy and prejudice? (Cite parallel examples, if you can.)

8. What do Mordecai and Esther each do about the evils perpetrated and planned against their people (Esther 3-5; 8)?

Questions for Application

This third set of questions is designed to bring the point home to yourself and other fathers.

9. Mordecai took a faith stand against public policy that was anti-Semitic, politically motivated, and personally humiliating (3:1-6). He wore sack cloth and wept and got others to join him in mourning. The threat of Haman's murderous anti-Semitism (4:1-3) drove Israel to its knees. Later, Mordecai started a petition drive (4:8) and organized a three-day, city-wide fast (4:15-17). Eventually he was appointed to public office where he had power to implement his own just policies (8:1-14). Esther, for her part, violated royal law and risked her life in taking her appeal to the top, but in her own charming, roundabout way (5:1-8; 7:1- 6; 8:3-6). By comparison, when you protest some policy or appeal some decision that you perceive as unjust, how do you go about it?

10. Can you envision, or have you experienced, a conflict of values that would threaten your job or worse?

In what circumstances would you stand firm?

What would make you soften your position?

11. What hope does "Mordecai's Day" (or Purim) give you that God is at work through institutions and individuals, to make your world a better place to raise children?

If you feel hopeless right now about your situation and need divine guidance, share and pray with your group of men. Reflect on Esther 4:14. How could God use you in "such a time as this"?

The Rest of the Story

Celebrating their deliverance from the oppressive enemy, the Jews under Mordecai went so wild that they did to their enemies what had been planned for them (Esther 9:1-16). The joyous but vengeful Jews turned the tables on the Amalekites, killing more and more each day in a merciless holy war (take no prisoners, take no booty). "And they did what they pleased to those who hated them" (9:5).

This R-rated part of the Mordecai story is hard to understand and apply from a New Testament perspective. The holy war that ensued (8:11) seems like unwarranted "ethnic cleansing" today. Clearly, such actions committed today are immoral public policy and unmitigated evil.

The Crusades, patterned after this bleak chapter in Mordecai's story, won a few battles against the infidels in the Middle Ages. Yet the Church is still reaping the bitter fruit of revenge and is in danger of losing the war for souls among Muslim and Jewish groups with long memories. King Xerxes' vengeful policy, implemented once Mordecai and Esther gained the upper hand, does not square with Jesus' words about "loving your enemy," "doing good to those who hate you" and "praying for those who persecute you" (Luke 6:27-36).

Nonetheless, Mordecai is a hero of the faith and my nominee for "patron saint of adoptive fathers." With Mordecai-like faith, we fathers can also make a difference in our families—one child at a time, one generation at a time, even "one nation under God" in His time.

Our Next "Dad of the Week"

The story of Mordecai and his behind-the-scenes work for the salvation of the Jews brings us, in due time (some 400 years later), to the salvation that Jesus would bring. A behind-the-scenes, legal guardian (but nonbiological father) also has a key role in this salvation story. I am, of course, referring to Joseph, stepfather of Jesus. I like to call him the "Patron Saint of Neglected Stepfathers," as he takes a back seat in church history to Mary, the birth mother and primary parent.

In preparation for this next chapter on fathering, read Matthew 1—2; Luke 1—3; and Matthew 13:53-57. Then reflect on what it means to be a legal but nonbiological father who parents one who was not his own flesh and blood.

Endnotes

1. Source: *The Zondervan Pictorial Encyclopedia of the Bible* (Zondervan, Grand Rapids, Michigan: 1976), Volume One, article on "Adoption."

2. See Chapter 2, Part II, where Jacob pursues God's blessing for himself (Genesis 27; 32) and then gives this blessing to his sons (Genesis 48-49). Conspicuously absent from those receiving the blessing of Jacob was Dinah, his only daughter.

3. Source: *The Interpreter's Dictionary of the Bible* (Abingdon, Nashville: 1954), Volume 3, page 840.

4. Good kids can come from bad or absentee parents. For example, the boy Josiah came from terribly evil fathers (Manasseh and Amon) and was orphaned at age eight, only to become Israel's great reformer-king (2 Kings 21-23). The apostle Paul taught as much when he said the children of only one believing parent can be sanctified, despite the harm done by an unbelieving parent (1 Corinthians 7:14-15).

—•••—

step•fa•ther, n: the husband of one's mother by a subsequent marriage.
step•son, n: a son of one's husband or wife by a former marriage.
Webster's Ninth (1983-)

—•••—

"Your children are not your children.
They are the sons and daughters of Life's longing for itself.
They come through you but not from you.
And though they are with you yet they belong not to you."
Kahlil Gibran, *The Prophet*

—•••—

CHAPTER TEN

Joseph and Other Neglected Stepfathers: Playing Second Fiddle to a Primary Parent

In pledging myself to you as a loyal husband,
I also pledge myself to becoming
as much of a father to your son Matt
as I am to my own two boys.

That was my uncompromising pledge, underscoring my wedding vows to Suzanne, Matt (then age 12), and my own two boys (Eric, then age 10, and Mark, then age 6). That vow came back to haunt me soon after we all five moved in together. In Matt's eyes, I fell from a welcome new supplemental dad. . . to a distrusted-because-I-play-favorites "jerk". . . to a spurned, unwanted intruder—all in twelve short months. (The much-ballyhooed honeymoon period only lasted three months.) Not loving Matt—as my own two boys—is what hurt Matt and Sue the most. Only now—four years into our life "together" (using the term loosely)—are we in recovery.

I mention this as an opening caveat, so you don't think I'm writing as an expert on stepfamilies. (My family knows better. See also question 9, page 121, which shows how little I knew starting out.) I also want to establish some ground with you noncustodial dads who may find yourself playing second fiddle to an primary parent."[1]

Yet I address this chapter to all dads. Understanding stepfamilies is vital because one-third of Americans now live in stepfamily relationships. That figure will grow to 50% during our lifetime.[2] Yet churches, schools, and other social agencies are only just beginning to understand the different needs and special characteristics of stepfamilies.[3]

The Dilemma of a Full-Time Dad and Second Fiddle Stepparent

I should back up a bit and give my readers some context for this stepparent's dilemma and failings. The death of my first marriage, several years prior, gave birth to my parenting skills and developed me as a nurturing father. As a single parent, of necessity I was a full-time dad *and* mom. (I say "full-time," although I had the welcome relief of trading off every other week with the boys' mom.) On weeks when I was the only on-duty parent, I parented full-time—doing all the housecleaning, grocery shopping, cooking, laundry, taxi service—all chores that once fell to my wife during my first marriage.

Ten years (to the day) after I became a first-time father, I became an instant stepfather. Little did I know then that just as one becomes a "real dad" in stages, so also "living in step" (stepparenting) happens only step by step, over a period of years.

When I married Suzanne, I declared my intention to become even more of a home-bound, "full-time" dad to our three sons. Since Sue is a career woman working as an interior designer, department manager, and account executive, and I work out of my home as a free-lance writer and editor, this arrangement made sense.

Behind every good intention, however, there looms a trouble spot. My wedding vow keeps me hanging in there when the going gets tough, but that's also what hangs me up. I am hooked on the horns of a dilemma familiar to most stepfathers: *I am eagerly wanted and stroked as a full-time father by my natural sons, who see me only every other week; but I was unwanted and rejected as any kind of father figure by my stepson.* (For two years he wanted me out of the picture so it could be just him and his mom, the way it was before.)

To Eric and Mark, I am a go-full-tilt-on-the-ballfield dad, . . . a share-all-your-feelings dad, . . . a let's-do-all-our-chores-together dad, . . . a read-the-bedtime-story-and-say-our-prayers dad. I'm even the type who gives hugs, kisses and high-fives whenever I greet my kids.

To Matt, such "touchy-feely" behavior and "let's-talk-it- out" invitations were "gross" and not at all "manly." I lost lots of ground those first two years, but after repenting of my ways and re-earning his trust, I'm gaining ground. This has not been easy. My turf for getting close to boys has been sports and Christianity, but Matt does not share those interests at all. I still struggle to find common ground and a place in his life. But my attitude has changed: I treasure him for being the son of the woman I love and for being the conscientious worker, entrepreneur, and college-bound 4.0-student that he is. While the pride and joy of his mother, I must admit, Matt is still somewhat of a mystery to me. He often defies my love and logic.

I also sense that Joseph, husband of Mary and stepfather to Jesus, knew what it was like to play second fiddle to a primary parent and cope with the mystery of a unique, hard-to-figure-out son. Joseph is a stepfather in that his son is one not of his own flesh and blood. Let us uncover what we can about this most neglected stepfather.[4]

A "CONSPIRACY OF SILENCE" SURROUNDING JOSEPH?

There's no doubt in my mind that Joseph of Nazareth earns the dubious distinction of "Most Forgotten Father" in Scripture. What little we know about this Joseph is gleaned from the scant press he gets from Matthew and Luke, or terse references to "the carpenter's son" (Matthew 13:55) or "Joseph's son" (Luke 4:22). These might even be posthumous references. Joseph is not mentioned at all in Mark's Gospel, and only indirectly in John's Gospel (6:42; 7:27-28). Joseph of Nazareth receives no mention in a classic, 1128-page Bible dictionary I own.[5]

Such silence by the patriarchal writers, early Church Fathers and current theologians is noteworthy. This conspiracy of silence supports our argument that Joseph is a forgotten father of his day. He becomes a forerunner of today's noncustodial dads who are often relegated by the courts and schools to a subsidiary and insignificant role in their children's lives.

But wait, . . . there's more to this conspiracy theory. According to Matthew, Joseph was a son of David and a man of integrity, honor and loyalty (Matthew 1:18-25). But not the biological father of Jesus. It is most intriguing for divorced dads and dads in paternity actions to know that Joseph, had he wished, could have denied paternity and filed for divorce without being liable for child support.

So righteous is Joseph that he chose to quietly divorce his fiancé Mary, as she carried a child not his.[6] A "quiet divorce" (one involving just two other witnesses) would have been more merciful to Mary than a full-blown court action. Joseph, wanting to do the right and merciful thing, did not want to publicly disgrace her.

He was later talked out of this divorce option by an angel—a true ***guardian ad litem***, if there ever was such a child's advocate in Scripture. Who but an angel could foresee that the best interests of the child to be born would include a continuing relationship with a father? This angelic priority is often absent in contemporary family courts. Many divorced or absentee dads need such "guardians" (whether divinely-appointed angels or court-appointed lawyers) who define and honor this "best interest of the child" principle to preserve the essential father-child bond.

Luke goes even further than Matthew to show that Joseph is not the biological father of Jesus. "Jesus...was the son of Joseph, *or so it was thought,* of Joseph" (emphasis mine, Luke 3:23). Luke's genealogy (3:23-38) differs from Matthew's (1:2-16) in several respects, especially from King David to the present. Luke's listing reflects the line of Mary (Jesus' ***blood relative***), whereas Matthew traces that of Joseph (Jesus' ***legal guardian***).[7]

The Roman Catholic church's treatment of Joseph is equally intriguing. In their veneration of Mary as "virgin mother," they have had to displace Joseph's obvious fatherhood. Catholic writers have expunged all biblical references to Joseph as the father of any children by Mary. According to Catholic sources, Joseph not only had no sex with Mary in producing Jesus, but Mary remained a virgin all her life.

Such Catholic tradition has to ignore, delete or reinterpret the many biblical references to the brothers of Jesus (Matthew 12:46; Mark 3:31; John 2:12; 7:3; 1 Corinthians 9:5; Galatians 1:19) and the one reference to his sisters (Matthew 13:55)—all presumably fathered by Joseph. To account for Jesus' "brothers and sisters," some theorize they were half-siblings, Joseph's children from a previous marriage. If so, why aren't all ten of the Joseph clan in our Christmas card manger scenes? (On the other hand, with an entourage of eight kids and a pregnant wife, no wonder "there was no room for them at the inn!")

This reasoning is clearly faulty. A more plausible, long-standing Protestant tradition holds that Joseph was the father of eight kids altogether—the four sons named in Matthew 13:55, plus four anonymous daughters. All eight were born *after* Jesus. Ironically, having numerous children, not "virgin motherhood" or "absent fatherhood," is what makes Mary and Joseph typical of and helpful to many Catholic parents today.

Joseph: Full-fledged but "Most Forgotten Father"?

Joseph was not the biological father of Jesus. He was, however, a father to Jesus in the legal or custodial sense. He did all the things that first century, full-time custodial dads did. Joseph took Jesus to Jerusalem for the rite of purification or circumcision at the prescribed time (Luke 2:21-39). Joseph protected Jesus, fleeing with his family to Egypt. They were an intercontinental political refugee family, forced from Asia to Africa by the wrath and murderous intent of King Herod (Matthew 2).[8]

After years spent as refugees, Joseph returned with his family to Nazareth of Galilee. There he mentored his son(s) in the family business of carpentry. The devout Joseph also took his family each year to Jerusalem for the Passover.

Protestant and Catholic traditions agree on this much: Joseph was almost certainly not alive during the adult ministry of Jesus. Mary and Jesus' brothers are mentioned, but Joseph is conspicuously absent (Matthew 12:46; 13:55; Mark 3:31; 6:3; John 9:26-27). He was almost certainly dead before his first-born son reached the age of thirty. That would explain why Joseph was overshadowed by Mary and overlooked by the Gospel writers and Church Fathers, who focused almost entirely on Jesus' adult life and public ministry (age 30-33).

Joseph caught only confusing glimpses of his adopted Son's life and ministry. Upon presenting the infant Jesus at the temple for circumcision and dedication to God, Joseph and Mary were told by Simeon and the prophetess Anna that Jesus would figure in the salvation of God's people (Luke 2:21-38). On another occasion, Jesus, at age twelve, confounded the elders by skipping out on the family's trip home. He chose instead to stay at the temple and talk theology with the rabbis (Luke 2:41-50)! His parents "did not understand what Jesus was saying to them."

However, Joseph of Nazareth must have been quite a father—to Jesus and to a quiver full of other children. How much of Jesus' personality and character reflected the inner spirit of Joseph? We can only speculate. He was a very supportive husband and instrument of God, as well. Joseph could see that "Jesus grew in wisdom and stature, and in favor with God and man" (Luke 2:52). Yet he would not live to see the fulfillment of his fathering. How sad and ironic that this father had only a veiled and partial understanding of the nature and mission of the Son he was rearing.

Other fathers die before giving away their sons and daughters in marriage or seeing them win at life. Joseph's death compounds the tragedy, since it served to veil our understanding of this key founding father! The absence of Joseph's story has robbed dads (and all believers) of a rich legacy of hope and faith.

For all the above-stated reasons, I nominate Joseph of Nazareth as our "Most Forgotten Father" and the "Patron Saint of Neglected Stepfathers." Is there a second to that nomination? Any further discussion?

Questions for Group Warm-up

These get-acquainted questions can be answered without reading the thematic introduction or doing the Bible study for this chapter.

1. Recall your decision to become a father. What factors went into your decision to enter fatherhood?

- ☐ We got pregnant out of wedlock, so the decision was made for us, by our "untimely" firstborn.
- ☐ I sensed a call, as if from an angel, that I was to be a dad.
- ☐ I'm not sure; it must have been an "immaculate conception."
- ☐ Conceiving the kids was easy; being a real dad has been hard.
- ☐ When I married my wife, I got an instant family.
- ☐ Our basic education was complete, our finances secure, and her biological clock ticking, so we finally got around to it.
- ☐ We've had problems getting pregnant, so I'm still not a dad.
- ☐ I have *always* wanted kids (all the fun, the perks, the adoration), but disdained the sacrifices necessary to be a real dad.
- ☐ I read this book and wanted to be one of those "fathers who made a difference."
- ☐ Other (please explain):

2. Some say, "A stepfamily is like an intact family, only with a few more kids, that's all." Do you agree? Why or why not? (Of the stepfamilies you know, what makes them qualitatively different from intact families?)

Questions for Bible Study

Read Matthew 1—2 and Luke 1—3. Then continue your group study by individually answering these questions and sharing with others from your notes.

3. What differences do you notice between the infancy narratives of Luke and of Matthew in the role they depict for Joseph?

4. How do you account for the differences in the two genealogy lists of Luke (3:23-38) and of Matthew (1:2-16). . . .

   a. as to the order of their lists?

   b. as to the man at the top of their list?

   c. as to the grandfather(s) and great-grandfather(s) of Jesus? (Which ancestral list do you work off of if you want to invite the clan to Jesus' *bar mitzvah*?)

5. Is the Virgin Birth necessary to the Gospel story? If so why?

   ☐ Joseph needed some face-saving way to avoid divorcing his betrothed.
   ☐ It was necessary to fulfill biblical prophecy (see Isaiah 7:14).
   ☐ I do *not* think the Virgin Birth is essential; Mark and John did not mention it.
   ☐ The virgin birth of Jesus is not unique to Christianity; even the Muslim's Koran attests to this particular doctrine.
   ☐ Other (please explain):

6. Given the scenario of Joseph as a "Most Forgotten Father," what do you think was the toughest, least appreciated part of what he did?

   ☐ Buying the line that Mary was not pregnant by another man, but by the Holy Ghost.
   ☐ Taking custody of "someone else's kid."
   ☐ Rearing a child under the fear of violence and pain of forced migration.
   ☐ Not having any sex with Mary until after Jesus was born.
   ☐ Having to answer critics who doubted the paternity of Jesus.
   ☐ Having to play second fiddle to the mother of Jesus.
   ☐ Having to support a wife and nine kids on a carpenter's salary.
   ☐ Not being able to see the fulfillment of his fathering.
   ☐ Having a "conspiracy of silence" draped over his coffin for centuries.

7. What do you think is the lasting legacy of Joseph?

Questions for Application

This third set of questions is designed to bring the point home to yourself and other fathers.

8. The lineage of Jesus was traced by Matthew to Abraham, and by Luke to Adam. How many generations back can you trace your lineage? (Who in your group can identify roots extending back on both the mother's side and father's side? to an immigrant who first came over on a boat? to a veteran of the Revolutionary War? to the Pilgrims? further back?)

b. (**Extra credit**) Jesus's family tree included women of foreign descent, on their second (or more) marriages, or renowned for scandal. Matthew notes the widowed Tamar, the Canaanite harlot Rahab, the widowed Moabitess Ruth, and the adulterous Bathsheba (1:3-6). Can you trace your lineage from any of the branches of your family tree that may have been cut off by divorce or death and/or grafted in by adultery or (re)marriage? Use a separate sheet of paper for this.

9. (**Just for fun**) Try answering the following six quiz questions taken from an actual stepfamily questionnaire. Mark the following statements True or False. ("Correct" answers are provided in the endnotes.)[9]

_____ **a.** Stepparents need to try to become close to stepchildren early in the relationship. Once too much time has elapsed, close relationships won't form.

_____ **b.** The most effective stepparents are those who assume the role of another parent figure in stepchildren's lives.

_____ **c.** Most children who have lived in a single-parent family long for sisters and brothers and welcome this aspect of their parent's remarriage.

_____ **d.** Stepfamilies move through specific, predictable stages.

_____ **e.** Although it takes time for love to develop between stepparents and stepchildren, this must happen sooner or later before the stepfamily can stabilize.

_____ **f.** A major difference between successful traditional nuclear families and successful stepfamilies is that, in the stepfamily, the couple's relationship often needs to be put on hold while children's needs and problems are resolved.

10. Support groups can strengthen stepfamilies. One support group identified five common sources of stress and eight reducers of stress. Which of these have you experienced in your families?

Build Stress 5 Ways

- ☐ Lack of recognition.
- ☐ Lack of affection.
- ☐ Lack of acceptance.
- ☐ Lack of control.
- ☐ No time off.

Reduce Stress 8 Ways

- ☐ Focus on the practical.
- ☐ Acts "as if" you felt a certain way (feelings follow actions).
- ☐ Refuse to get into arguments.
- ☐ Accept responsibility for only your actions.
- ☐ Find support systems.
- ☐ Let go of things not in your control (like trying to "fix" an ex-spouse).
- ☐ Let others have responsibility for their own actions.
- ☐ Date your mate regularly and spontaneously.

The Rest of the Story

Joseph's story, of course, is unlike that of most stepparents, in that he had no ex-spouse to complicate custody and visitation schedules, etc. Yet he joined all stepfathers who *know* our stepchild is not *of* us, nor *by* us, nor *through* us. Joseph even knew, as all stepdads know, that sometimes teenage stepchildren will not want anything to do *with* us. Still, stepfathers have a part to play in their stepchild's life—a role less significant than that of a biological parent, perhaps, but important nonetheless.

Joseph remained faithful to God, Mary and Jesus. God's reward to Joseph was the gift any parent most desires: his precious stepson became a righteous man, obedient to God. Their story gives us all hope that God will do as much for parents who believe God's messengers, trust His mysterious ways, and persevere, whether or not we see our parenting bear fruit. As Joseph did, so can we.

Our Next "Dad of the Week"

Not every child returns home "obedient to his parents," as did the 12-year-old Jesus (Luke 2:51). Some run away to sow their wild oats, like the legendary Prodigal Son. In preparation for this next chapter on fathering, read Luke 15:11-32; then reflect on what it means to be a "Parent of a Prodigal."

Endnotes

1. The *primary* (or "preferred") parent in stepfamily situations could be your *ex-spouse* (custodial parent, 85% of time is the mother), your *new spouse* (and parent of your stepchildren), and/or her *ex-spouse* (your stepchildren's other biological parent).

2. "Understanding Stepfamilies" by Jan Larson, *American Demographics* (July 1992). Also cited in current publications of the American Stepfamily Association of America (Lincoln, Nebraska). More information is available from that group by calling its toll-free number, 1-800/735-0329. For more detailed census information on stepfamilies, see "Married-Couple Families with Children" by Louisa F. Miller and Jeanne E. Moorman, *Current Population Reports*, Series P-23, No. 162, available from the Census Bureau.

3. Agreeing on methods and responsibility for discipline and nurturance; merging family rituals for the holidays; scheduling joint vacations and visits; settling policy on privacy and space needs, weekly allowance and household chores; resolving loyalty conflicts and control issues with the other parent—all that (and a whole lot more!) goes into understanding and forging a new family unit out of two previous marriages with children.

4. This caveat should be noted: Joseph fits Webster's definition of a stepfather to Jesus in two respects: (1) Joseph was "the husband of Jesus' mother," and; (2) Joseph's marriage to Mary was subsequent to Jesus' birth. However, Jesus does not perfectly fit Webster's definition of stepson. Jesus was not the son of Joseph's wife "by a former marriage." In keeping with orthodox Christian tradition, we can safely say Jesus was born of Mary *to* Joseph by divine agency (Matthew 3:17; Luke 1:32-35; Hebrews 1:5). Thus, Jesus was not *of* Joseph, nor *by* Joseph. See also Kahlil Gibran's opening quote for a sense of this peculiar father-child relationship, with which virtually all stepfathers can identify.

5. Joseph, the eleventh son of Jacob, gets all the press under the "Joseph" entry in *Nelson's Illustrated Bible Dictionary* (Thomas Nelson Publishers, Nashville: 1986).

6. Engagement was as binding as marriage in those days. Unfaithfulness during engagement was regarded as adultery. Because the engagement was binding, divorce was the only honorable, face-saving way out.

7. *The NIV Study Bible* (Zondervan, Grand Rapids, Michigan: 1985). Such genealogies were compiled for the New Testament to address questions of Jesus' paternity that persisted all of Joseph's life, Mary's life, and well into the period of the early church.

8. I am indebted to my mentor, Dr. Raymond Bakke, of the Chicago-based International Urban Associates, for this insight into Jesus as an "intercontinental political refugee."

9. *Strengthening Stepfamilies* (c) 1986 American Guidance Service, Inc., Circle Pines, MN. All Rights reserved. Used with permission. Excerpted here are only six of the 30 questions in their quiz, "What I Believe about Stepfamily Living." However, these six questions are the ones yours truly got wrong and my beloved got all right. (I scored 80% overall.) Shows you who knows more! Check yourself against these correct answers: a=F, b=F, c=F, d=T, e=F, f=F.

—•••—

prod•i•gal, *adj* **1:** recklessly extravagant; **2:** characterized by a wasteful expenditure : lavish; **3:** yielding abundantly: luxuriant. **syn** see profuse
prod•i•gal, *n:* one who spends or gives lavishly and foolishly.
Webster's Ninth (1983-)

—•••—

"Every parent is at some time the father of the unreturned prodigal with nothing to do but keep his house open to hope."
John Ciardi (1916-1986)

—•••—

"Let a man go away or come back; God never leaves. He is always at hand, and if he cannot get into your life, still he is never farther away than the door."
Meister Eckhart (c.1260—c.1327)

—•••—

CHAPTER ELEVEN

The Waiting Father and Other Fathers of Prodigals: Hoping for a Re Pain of Childlessness

We all know the Prodigal Son. He is us. He is in us, our inner child. He is our problem teenager, our freedom-loving friend. He is Everyman.

We also know the Elder Brother. He too is us and in us. He is our nagging conscience. He is our dutiful, conscientious worker. He is the standard of obedience to which we hold ourselves and others.

We are also called to receive from and become like the Waiting Father. We are to mirror God's unconditional love to rebellious sinners and self-righteous sons alike, to all God's children.

Let's look at the man in the mirror by the light of this parable. Perhaps we'll see different reflections of ourselves, our loved ones, and our calling more clearly.

The prodigal son phase

He is our inner child who *must* cut loose from his father, get into a few scrapes of his own, and wriggle out of them.

He is our teenager, the freedom-lover, who *must* sow his wild oats, find his true identity and prove his manhood—apart from his parents.

He is the adventurous one who *must* try his own wings away from home for the first time, to bum around and explore before settling down.

He is the pleasure-seeker who *must* instantly gratifiy his every desire, who makes a lot, spends a lot, loses a lot—as if there were no tomorrow.

He is our extravagant, arrogant self, eager to explore the world, gain popularity, success, and wealth, only to come to grief, misfortune, or even a disastrous mid-life crisis along the way.

Everyone shares the "oughta-gotta-shoulda" feelings at some time. The passionate feeling may or may not compel us to act. However, someone who truly *must* do such things, is no longer *free!* He is *bound* by his desires to gratify them. He is *bound* by his extravagant spending ways to keep up pretense, to fake it until he makes it. He his *bound* by his neediness and homesickness to continually amuse himself with diversions.

His behavior is also *bound* to go from good to bad to worse, from riches to rags, from fine fare to swine fare, from anxious moments to fearful days to wasted years. This spiral continues and his conscience convicts, unabated, until worry ties him up in knots. This downward spiral *must* rob him of his freedom, and enslaves him to other masters. He may even sell his soul, unless he repents or comes "to his senses" (Luke 15:17).

The prodigal son phase, as with other phases of life, is not tied to a distinct time and place. Leaving home is not just going away to college, cleaving to a wife, or setting up shop 1000 miles from hometown roots. If "home is where the heart is," and if home in Jesus' parable is wherever the heart of God brings us, then "leaving home" is about running away spiritually. Leaving home is ignoring the voice of God and heeding the voices of success, popularity and power. Leaving home is following the voices of temptation, addiction, and fear, instead of the voice of God in our hearts, in the counsel of Christian friends, and through Scripture.

While I left my Father's house (the church) for about five years, my adolescent choices were prodigal-like. So was the period of my "second adolescence" during my "single-again thirties." I behaved like the prodigal every time I hungered for The Blessing that only a true father can give. Prodigal-like feelings of darkness, disillusionment, or despair still overwhelm me at times. Then I come to my senses, and I sense I am not alone.

At such moments, I need to reclaim my sonship. I must recall the sense of worth that comes from being a child of God, forever welcome in my Father's arms. When I base my sense of worth on my bank account, the fickle reactions of friends or my fleeting accomplishments at work, I must come to my senses, like the Prodigal, and return to my Father. Not only will the Father be waiting, but He can even redeem the inheritance we squandered. That's Good News for anyone who grows up insecure!

Jesus became like the Prodigal for us. Although Jesus never rebelled or disobeyed the Father, he still walked the Prodigal's path. He left his heavenly home, took a humiliating journey to a distant land, suffering extreme indignity and guilt. His prodigal story is all the more poignant because it was *our* guilt Jesus carried, not his own. The Savior Prodigal returned home through the Cross to bring his lost prodigal brothers and sisters back to waiting arms of God the Father.[1]

THE ELDER BROTHER PHASE

When I look honestly at the man in the mirror, I see the elder brother as well as the prodigal son. I was born first in my family and enjoyed all the usual perks, duties and expectations of the firstborn male. I assumed responsible leadership positions on every club, class and team I joined. I was the top graduating male student, the senior class president, the football co-captain, and the student voted "Most Likely to Succeed."

My résumé said "elder brother" all over it, but my inner child was screaming like the "Prodigal Son." Despite my success in the classroom and football field, I felt empty, insecure and unhappy. In college I floundered through five declared majors and several girlfriends, trying to find myself and someone to love me.

I later understood that I was associating parental or peer approval and praise with achievement and praiseworthy performance. I didn't know I could be accepted for who I was, even if I failed at love, advanced calculus, or collegiate-level sports. I didn't know unconditional love until I heard and felt the Father's reassuring words, "My son."

Still, becoming a Christian did not keep me from holding onto the hard-working, duty-bound, morally intense Elder Brother identity. I immediately pursued vocational Christian service, working 80 hours a week. This only brought out more of the self-righteous Pharisee within me. Fourteen years later, my world came crashing down. I was separated from my family and the job I loved; I came to God with my brokenness. I felt unworthy of His all-forgiving love, but He healed me.

Now and again my elder brother mentality still flares up, such as when I work hard to please someone but feel unappreciated. Like the elder brother in the story ("Yet you never gave me.... But when this son of yours...."), I'm prone to compare, complain and keep score.

Whether you and I are more like the younger son or the older brother, we are all called to become like the all-forgiving father.

The "Prodigal Father"

Traditionally, the word *prodigal* communicates "lost" or "wayward." Words like "reckless" and "extravagant" come to mind. But by Webster's definition (and Ken Canfield's insight), the son in this parable is *not* the only one who is "recklessly extravagant," "lavish," or "luxuriant." So is the father in this story. Some call him *the* "prodigal father."[2]

On the long road back to his father, the prodigal son was not exactly traveling light. He was burdened by a sense of accountability and ambiguity. "Perhaps," the son might have reasoned, "if my extenuating circumstances and excuses are plausible, I'll receive a light sentence, hard labor and time off for good behavior." Instead, the prodigal father gave him nothing less than absolute, unconditional, mind-boggling, sin-cleansing, penalty-canceling forgiveness.

This unexpected twist in the story line was meant for Jesus' original audience, a crowd of Pharisees and common folks. The original hearers would have objected, as did the elder brother, to the father lavishing grace upon grace. Instead of dishing out the deserved justice or expected retribution, the father threw a party (Luke 15:22-24). Instead of exacting an apology or proper penance, the father went the extra mile: He ran to meet the son, embraced him, and brought a special robe, ring, and sandals for him. In a further gesture that must have seemed wasteful or "prodigal" to some, the father even killed the fattened calf, and invited hordes of people for a wedding-like feast, complete with joyous music and dancing. Talk about "prodigal" spending!

In its historical context, the Prodigal Son story is quite offensive. To request an inheritance *before* the father's death was, in effect, wishing the father dead.[3] What an unthinkable, mean-spirited request! Most fathers would punish such arrogance. Instead, the father in this story honors the audacious request and gives his son exactly what he requested.

The inheritance was given, not loaned. There was no "living trust" proviso to support the father in his old age. Nor were there any questions asked or any strings attached. It was an act of pure extravagance—gracious or foolish, but recklessly excessive indeed.

A joyous homecoming party is in full swing when the elder brother arrives. He is furious, hurt. He does not understand his wayward brother nor his forgiving father (15:30). His aloofness, anger, and resentment stand in sharp contrast to the father's warmth and acceptance. Yet the extravagance of the father's love extends to this son, as well: "My son. . .you are always with me and everything I have is yours" (15:31).

The father reaches out but does not force. Though he knew the elder brother was trapped in self-pity and sibling rivalry of his own making, the father loved him uniquely and honored his obedience. The obedient son was invited to more than a party; he was invited out of himself, to be more trusting, joyous, grateful, and free. All that the father had was his. The elder son had no need for competition, envy, or resentment.

The compassionate father saw both his sons realistically, and so could empathize and give them the love they needed. Here then is a universal father-son story. We can all identify.

Questions for Group Warm-up

These get-acquainted questions can be answered without reading the thematic introduction or doing the Bible study for this chapter.

1. Draw a time line below (or on a blank page). Identify points when you were operating in any of three roles: the *younger son* role, the *elder brother* role, and the *waiting father* role. (Hint: Include not just your physical leave-taking, but any spiritual leave-taking and homecoming. Identify the symbolic "distant country" and the "home base" that represent the tug of opposing values. Identify turning points God used to bring you to Himself or to incline your heart fully toward home.

Questions for Bible Study

Read Luke 15:11-32. Then continue your group study by individually answering these questions and sharing with others from your notes.

2. Which of the following fit the image of
- the Prodigal Son? (place a **PS** in the blank)
- the Elder Brother? (place a **EB** in the blank)
- the Waiting Father? (place a **WF** in the blank)

(Hint: You can use any of these descriptive phrases more than once.)

___ think ahead, act later
___ impulsive
___ traditional
___ far-sighted
___ approval-seeking
___ lavish
___ responsible
___ jealous
___ rule-bound
___ freedom-bound
___ homebound
___ always home
___ coming home broke(n)
___ lost
___ died many deaths
___ dead to life, unfeeling
___ far away from God
___ asks no questions
___ presumptuous
___ common sense
___ uncommon charity
___ self-loathing
___ got what he deserved
___ running away
___ sitting alone
___ thrill-seeking

___ act now, think later
___ delayed gratification
___ adventuresome
___ near-sighted
___ freedom-loving
___ foolish
___ irresponsible
___ greedy
___ sin-bound
___ all bound up
___ home-sick
___ sick of home
___ homecoming parade
___ homecoming party-pooper
___ alive with life
___ mean-spirited death-wish
___ closest to God
___ full of questions
___ principled
___ came to his senses
___ self-absorbed
___ self-righteous
___ did not got what he deserved
___ running toward
___ standing aloof
___ searching for significance

3. The Parable of the Prodigal Son has lost some impact over the years because of its familiarity. When the story was first told, the audience of Pharisees and common people expected a more traditional ending. How would you rewrite the script with

more traditional dialogue between the father and *younger* son, once the son "came to his senses"?

- ☐ The son came home, saying, "I've made a man of myself; now that I've matured you can take me back."
- ☐ The son confessed, "I've run out of money, Dad. Could you split the inheritance once more so I can start over again?"
- ☐ The father can't help but rub it in: "I told you so! See what you've been missing? Now if only you. . . ."
- ☐ The son shrugged off his wanderlust, "I got sick of living high off the hog; I guess Dad's place isn't so bad, after all."
- ☐ The father hides out, plays hard to pacify, and must be won over by the groveling and plea bargaining of a desperate son.
- ☐ Justice and retribution prevail; the son gets what he deserves.
- ☐ Not wanting to enable his son's bad decisions, the father says, "I accept your apology and invite you to join my farm hands as an employee."
- ☐ Other (please explain):

4. How would you rewrite the script with a more traditional dialogue between the father and *elder* son, once the younger son returned home?

- ☐ The elder brother decides it doesn't pay to be good and so goes on a fling of his own.
- ☐ The elder brother never enters into the joy but dies a bitter man.
- ☐ The father and son engage in a battle of wills, as neither has enough trust to relinquish a claim on the other.
- ☐ Any ending but the open-ended one which just keeps the audience hanging, wondering if the elder brother ever reconciled.
- ☐ Other (please explain):

5. This parable primarily teaches about the heavenly Father's grief-bearing, all-forgiving love. Yet this parable also offers insight into sonship and fatherhood on an earthly plane. What object lessons can you take away for your role as a father or son?

QUESTIONS FOR APPLICATION

This third set of questions is designed to bring the point home to yourself and other fathers.

6. What Prodigal Son experiences have you had?

What Elder Brother experiences have you had?

What Waiting Father experiences have you had?

7. You may have trouble identifying with the Prodigal, especially if you did not leave home, run around with loose women or face despair or bankruptcy. Still, a prodigal can think back with gratitude to all God has forgiven him. What about your life now or your life before you turned it over Christ, resembles the life of a prodigal? (Remember, we often experience forgiveness to the depth of our confession.)

8. You may have had trouble identifying with the father who was quick to forgive, unconditional in his acceptance, extravagant his grace, and exuberant in his joy. Why might that be?

- ☐ I have failed to forgive those who have wronged me.
- ☐ I don't understand the father who raised me any more than Jesus' original audience understood this incredible father.
- ☐ I don't have that kind of compassion to give others; I need it for myself.
- ☐ I can't appreciate the father's role because I've experienced God's justice and power overshadowing the tender touch of His love and mercy.
- ☐ I hate sin, especially those who have sinned against me, and I can't imagine ever forgiving them.
- ☐ Other (please explain):

9. The human heart has its reasons for withholding forgiveness, some of which are suggested below. Which reasons apply where you find it hardest to forgive?

- ☐ The offense was simply too great.
- ☐ The offender has shown no remorse and offered no apology.
- ☐ The offending party wasn't truly sorry; the "excuse" was a sham.
- ☐ The offense was deliberate, provocative, likely to occur again.
- ☐ To forgive the offender is to take responsibility for his or her rehabilitation, which I cannot do.
- ☐ I may be able to forgive, but I'll never forget.
- ☐ If I forgive once, I'll have to again; my forgiveness is limited.
- ☐ I've buried the hatchet and what's done is done; I'd rather not face or reconcile with the offender, much less become friends.
- ☐ How can I forgive if I can't trust this person?
- ☐ Other (please explain):

10. Some of you have yet to claim your sonship. You need your heart turned toward home, to reconcile with your father and/or to receive your Heavenly Father's blessing. Others of you have yet to claim your fatherhood. And so you need to turn your heart toward home, to be a more compassionate, accepting father who really enjoys his children, even the errant ones. Which is the case for you and what do you need to do about that?

11. The Prodigal Son is Everyman's story. Yet the parents of prodigals each suffer in their own way, at depths only the Man of Sorrows can fully understand. What pain have you suffered as the parent of a prodigal?

Conversely, reflect on the pain you may have caused your own father. In what sense are you the son of a "prodigal father"?

Close in prayer by bringing to the Father your collective experiences of pain, guilt, and anger, as well as your desires for reconciliation.

The Rest of the Story

Jesus' parable, in Luke's context, invites us to rejoice. The shepherd rejoices at finding lost sheep (15:6), the woman at finding her lost coin (15:9), and the father at finding his lost son (15:24,32). Angels of God rejoice with every sinner who repents (15:7,10).

The point is this: *God embraces sinners, rejoices in forgiving us, and invites us to share in that joy-filled life with Him and with others.* The elder brother is faced with a choice between resentment and joy. So also are the Pharisees, who listened to Jesus tell these three parables (Luke 15:1-2). This parable is for anyone reluctant to have fellowship with sinners.

The invitation to joy is the call of sonship. If we obey God's commandments and remain in His love, the joy of Jesus will be in us and that joy will be complete (John 15:9-11). And the call to sonship is a first step toward becoming a compassionate father who calls still other sons to share in his joy.

Our Next "Dad of the Week"

The next chapter extends this theme of fathering to spiritual reproduction, mentoring, and discipleship. The book of Acts and the letters of Paul depict two and three generations of fathering or mentoring relationships between Barnabas, Paul, Timothy, and other faithful men.

In preparation, read Acts 9:26-30; 11:22-30; 16:1-5; 1 Corinthians 4:14-17; 2 Timothy 1:1-7; 2:1-7. Reflect on what it means to be a "Father in Christ" to young disciples.

Endnotes

1. For this theological insight, I am indebted to Henri Nouwen, who offers this nontraditional interpretation in his book, *The Return of the Prodigal Son* (Doubleday, New York: 1992).

2. Ken Canfield, of National Center for Fathering (Shawnee Mission, Kansas), shares this insight in his magazine, *Today's Father*, Vol. 2, No. 2, 1994.

3. For this historical insight, I am also indebted to Henri Nouwen, in *The Return of the Prodigal Son* (Doubleday, New York: 1992).

—•••—

fa•ther: a husband who has accepted the discipleship responsibility for his children.

David DeWitt, *The Mature Man*

—•••—

"One father is worth more than a hundred schoolmasters."

George Herbert (1593-1633)

—•••—

"Nothing that is worth knowing can be taught."

Oscar Wilde (1854-1900)

—•••—

CHAPTER TWELVE

Paul and Other "Fathers in Christ": Mentoring and Passing on the Faith

Men who father others never lose their own need for someone to "father" them. You may have been moved by the Prodigal Son story (Luke 15:11-32; see Chapter 11) to identify with the "prodigal father" and take a more compassionate, giving, patient or forgiving role in your children's life. For many men, this means stepping outside their comfort zone into areas where there are few role models, check points or support system. We want to follow through, yet we need a road map.

At the July 1993 Promise Keeper's National Men's Conference at Boulder, Colorado, I heard the challenge and call to spiritual fatherhood and mentoring relationships: *A Promise Keeper is committed to pursuing vital relationships with a few other men, understanding that he needs brothers to help him keep his promises.*

I have accepted the challenge issued there by the platform speaker Howard Hendricks to find a Barnabas, a Paul, and a Timothy in my life. I need someone to be my spiritual father (a Paul) and my spiritual brother (a Barnabas), as I seek to father a spiritual son (a Timothy). The mentor's creed, as expressed by Paul to Timothy (2 Timothy 2:1-2), applies, in turn, to us: "You then, my son, be strong in the grace that is in Christ Jesus. And the things you have heard me say in the presence of many witnesses entrust to reliable men who will also be qualified to teach others."

That mentor's creed—and the call to be a "father in Christ," as Paul was to Timothy, and a brother in Christ, as Barnabas was to Paul—is the focus of this study.

These father-brother-son relationships were pivotal in building the early church. Barnabas was to Paul a prayer partner, traveling companion, critical advocate, and soul brother. Barnabas held Paul accountable and supported his missionary endeavors. Paul was to Timothy a wise elder. He was further down the road on his spiritual journey and willing to come alongside a younger believer in a mentoring relationship. Timothy, in turn, was a young recruit and potential mentor in his own right. One day he would "entrust reliable men" with the gospel, men who would then "teach others also."

Finding a "Barnabas" to be your spiritual brother

Joseph of Cypress, raised a Levite, was a self-employed, wealthy landowner when he became a Christian. He made a significant gift of real estate to care for the poor and encourage the early church (Acts 4:37). That was the first of Joseph's long track record of deeds done to encourage others. Eventually, he was nicknamed Barnabas, meaning "Son of Encouragement" (4:36).

Barnabas could see the "grace of God" at work in other people (11:23-24), especially new Christians and future leaders of the church. He was a particular source of encouragement to Saul-turned-Paul.

Some believers distrusted and feared Saul. Barnabas instead broke ranks and welcomed this government agent who had been persecuting Christians. He chose to trust Saul and accept his conversion as genuine (Acts 9:26-27). Mr. Encouragement steered Saul into leadership of the early church when the time was right (11:25-26). When a new international team of leaders gathered for prayer, fasting and decision-making at Antioch, Barnabas ventured out with Saul, now called Paul, in a world missions thrust (13:1—14:28). When that persecutor-turned-preacher needed an advocate to protect him from critics, Barnabas was right there (15:1–4,12).

Barnabas did the same risky advocacy work for young John Mark. After quitting Paul's missionary team (12:25; 13:13), Mark was rejected for another assignment by Paul. Barnabas stepped into the prodigal father role and took John Mark with him (15:36-41). Restored to ministry by Barnabas' love and teaching, John Mark later proved "helpful" to Paul (2 Timothy 4:11) and is thought to have written one of the four Gospels.

Evidently, Barnabas could discern leadership potential where others could not. Barnabas epitomized a brother "strong in the grace that is in Christ Jesus" (2:1). Neither Paul nor John Mark nor the early church would have accomplished what they did without the encouragement of Barnabas. We stand with them in need of Barnabas-like encouragement to fulfill our calling as fathers and promise keepers.

Why "Timothy" needs "Paul" to be a spiritual father

As defined by David DeWitt and George Herbert (see opening quotes), true fathers are precious, few, and hard-to-find. That fact is well-documented in the school records, divorce courts, penal institutions, and welfare systems of our day. With a 1,420 percent hike in the divorce rate since 1920, fifteen million children are now growing up without any father in the home.[1] Many social ills—such as poor academic performance, increased truancy, poverty, welfare dependence, juvenile violence, gang warfare, and incarceration—have been attributed to the lack of a strong father presence in the home.

One statistic of the fatherless child stands out above all others in my mind. It validates my own ministry and is a key impetus behind this book and the whole Promise Keeper movement. Would you believe that when the father is an active Christian, his children are *five* times more likely to become Christians than when only the mother is a believer? Evidently, there is a 75% conversion rate when Dad is a spiritual father, compared to a mere 15% when Mom alone is a spiritual midwife.[2]

Timothy overcame these odds. His family was racially and religiously mixed. His father was a pagan Greek, and his mother and grandmother Jewish (Acts 16:1-3; 2 Timothy 1:5). Paul was his "father in Christ" and Timothy was Paul's "true son in the faith."[3] Paul recruited young Timothy. He tutored him, took him on various missionary trips and pastoral calls, and eventually appointed him to racially-mixed Ephesus (Acts 16:1-3; Philippians 2:19-23; 1 and 2 Timothy).

Once you find your Timothy, you will want to look for those kind of "teachable moments." You will use time and opportunities to begin the investment process, from your life into his.

Finding a "Teachable Moment" to Begin Your Mentoring Relationship

One teachable moment strengthened a mentoring relationship for me. As told to Glenn Wagner, and included in his chapter on mentoring relationships in *Seven Promises of a Promise Keeper*, here it is:

> I was due to be married in June [for the second time] but got cold feet and called it off one month before the wedding. My career in life insurance sales was also at a dead end. I had asked Dick, a seminary professor and sometime mentor over the years, to officiate at the wedding. Wanting to comfort me in my disappointment and to guide me in my ongoing search for meaningful work, Dick came out from Boston to Wisconsin on the weekend the wedding would have happened.
>
> As we shared heart to heart, Dick ended up inviting me to write for him. I changed careers to apprentice myself as a "Timothy" to this veteran communicator of the faith. That mentoring relationship has continued to this day, but it would not have begun [along this path of partnering in Bible projects] had it not been for a crisis of confidence.[4]

Not all teachable moments for starting up mentoring relationships must be life-changing experiences, like the one cited here. To jump-start your mentoring relationship, you and your Paul or Timothy must simply be open to change and acknowledge both gifts and needs. People are often most open or teachable when: (1) struggling through crisis; (2) overwhelmed by inadequacy; (3) confronted with a unresolved need or problem; (4) challenged or measured by a goal; or (5) searching for a more meaningful relationship.[5]

Age-appropriate learning activities can enable fathers to teach and instill values in children.[6] Team sports can teach discipline, self-sacrifice, and loyalty. Children can learn through sports to overcome fear, set high goals, and finish what they start. Don't discount so-called "dangerous activities," such as hunting, dirt-biking, and race-car driving. Fun and adventure with Dad also teaches wisdom, careful decision-making and environmental stewardship. Fun with youth leaders and friends is valuable, but Dad still has responsibility to model and instruct his children in faith and godly living.[7]

Will you be a Paul to a Timothy at work and home? Let's find out.

Questions for Group Warm-up

These get-acquainted questions can be answered without reading the thematic introduction or doing the Bible study for this chapter.

1. Consider your spiritual roots. Who are (or were) the praying people in your life that influence(d) your spiritual decision process?

What do you know about the faith commitment or religious affiliation of your forefathers and mothers?

2. Consider again the significant father figures in your life. Who was active in...

a. Leading you to Christ?

b. Shaping your Christ-like character?

c. Making you into a fruitful disciple of Christ?

3. Thanks to racial and ethnic intermarriage, few Americans are of only one ethnic origin. How far back can you trace the ethnic identity of your forefathers and mothers?

Questions for Bible Study

Read Acts 16:1-3; 1 Corinthians 4:1-17; 2 Timothy 1:1—2:7, 3:14-15. Then continue your group study by individually answering these questions and sharing with others from your notes.

4. Consider how Paul describes his life and ministry as a "father in Christ" (1 Corinthians 4:1-17). What aspects of his life and ministry does he urge the Corinthians (and us) to "imitate"?

5. Paul calls us to "imitate" him.[8] He also warns against following any one particular leader or father figure—not even Apollos, Peter or Paul is worthy of that (1 Corinthians 1:11-17). How do you resolve this apparent contradiction?

6. Consider the metaphors and analogies Paul used to motivate Timothy. Ask the Lord for insight as you reflect on them (2 Timothy 2:1-7).

a. In what respect is a spiritual father or disciple-maker like a *good soldier?*

b. . . .like a *competitive athlete?*

c. . . .like a *hard-working farmer?*

Questions for Application

This third set of questions is designed to bring the point home to yourself and other fathers.

7. Which of these descriptions of Paul (gleaned from 1 Corinthians 4:1-17), are true of you as a spiritual father, mentor, or disciple-maker?

- ☐ servant of Christ (4:1)
- ☐ preacher of the Gospel (4:1)
- ☐ track record of faithfulness (4:2)
- ☐ non-judgmental (4:3)
- ☐ clear conscience (4:4)
- ☐ patient (4:5)
- ☐ pure motives (4:5)
- ☐ humble (4:6)
- ☐ weak, vulnerable, or fragile (4:9,10)
- ☐ fool for Christ (4:10)
- ☐ lifestyle of poverty, hard-working, self-supporting (4:11,12)

- ☐ condemned, ridiculed, or dishonored by others (4:9,10)
- ☐ butt of jokes, abuse, scapegoating, or scorn (4:13)
- ☐ compassionate and stern, with his "dear children" (4:14)

b. Which of the above qualities of a "father in Christ" do you lack?

c. Which will you adopt in obedience to Paul's urging to *imitate* him (4:16)?

8. Paul makes a point of distinguishing between "*guardians* in Christ" and a "*father* in Christ" (1 Corinthians 4:15). Evidently, one father was preferable to thousands of guardians. But Paul never defines his terms. Several interpretations have been offered below, which may shed some light on why some mentoring relationships (with true *fathers*) last and while others (with *guardians*) do not. According to these possible definitions, which are you a "*guardian*" or a "*father*" in relation to those you mentor at home? at work? at church?

- ☐ Guardians are concerned with preserving the status quo, whereas fathers are concerned with growing (spiritual) children to maturity and faithful reproduction.
- ☐ Guardians are the missionaries and ministers who are patronized for the prestige and status they lend to various factions within the church.
- ☐ Fathers by definition are not self-centered, but other-focused, always looking out for the best interest of the child.
- ☐ Guardians are obtrusive intermediaries, with vested interests and layers of tradition that hinder knowing God firsthand.
- ☐ Guardians are like lax and naive babysitters, whereas fathers are stern and loving, able to admonish and correct behavior.
- ☐ Guardians are philosophers or wisdom-teachers who tickle people's fancies with the latest theories, whereas fathers are evangelists who take responsibility for their converts and urge obedience to the Gospel.
- ☐ Fathers are unique as founders who "begot" a certain work, whereas guardians are those who would build on another's foundational work.

9. Will you be a Barnabas, investing your life for the benefit of a future Saul or John Mark? (Be specific as to who and when.)

If you are *not* willing or eager to mentor young converts, why not?

10. (**Optional**) Paul nurtured Timothy through "father-son" letters (1 Timothy 1:2; 2 Timothy 1:2) that were very personal and pastoral. If you were to write a personal

and pastoral letter to your son or daughter, what Paul-like elements would you include? Helpful Hint: To help you outline this letter, imagine your child is going away for a long period of time (moving cross-country? military service?), taking on new levels of responsibility (marriage? management?), or entering new passages of parenthood. Picture yourself during significant changes (mid-life crisis? retirement? dying?). Reflect on those to your child through a letter.

The Rest of the Story

I once conducted an "interview," of sorts, with Timothy, the excerpts of which I offer as a postscript. Imagine such a marketplace profile of Timothy in a first century tabloid, the *Ephesus Times*. Ask yourself: Do I know anyone like this, a young believer whom I could disciple? (How well do you know your own children in this regard?)

My name means: "**Honored of God.**"
Hometown: **Lystra, where I heard the gospel on Paul's first missionary journey.**
Family: **I'm the product of a mixed marriage; Dad is Greek and Mom is Jewish (she later became a Christian), but my father in the faith is Paul.**
Profession: **I was a respected community leader in Lystra and Iconium when Paul made me a chief associate and project leader with him. Later was appointed bishop of Ephesus.**
I am best known as: **Paul's sidekick and the recipient of two of his pastoral letters.**
Best decision I ever made: **Joining up with Paul on his second missionary journey—it was even worth the pain of adult circumcision and some stints in Roman jails.**
Worst part of my job was: **Early on. Because of my youth, I couldn't get any respect.**
Worst time of my life: **My failure in Corinth. Paul had to warn them to go easy on me; he also named Titus (a more forceful personality), not me, as his apostolic delegate there.**
Behind my back my friends say: **I'm timid, fearful, sickly, even lustful.**
Three words which best describe me: **Sensitive, affectionate, loyal.**
If I could convince people of one thing, it'd be: **Stand fast in the face of affliction and complete, by grace, whatever is lacking in your faith.**
Just when the going got tough: **Paul had a more challenging task for me.**
If I have one regret in life, it is: **Not being there for Paul at the end when he needed me most.**
The "good ol' days" for me were when: **Paul and the others laid hands on me and I received a special endowment of the Holy Spirit for ministry I'll never forget.**

You get the gist of this interview: Get to know what makes your son tick. Find a need and meet it. I have no doubt there is a Timothy in your circles yearning to be fathered in the faith. To find that Timothy you might have to be creative and persistent. First consider the needs of your own extended family. Then look outside for some "dear son" with whom you can share your life as a supplemental or surrogate father. Check out Big Brother/Big Sister programs, the Scouts, Sunday school, confirmation class, youth groups, community clubs, hobby organizations, recreational leagues, the local YMCA, or neighborhood associations.

Once you find your Timothy, you'll find yourself asking, "What would an elder like Paul do for a young protégé like Timothy?" You'll then act like a real nurturing father, blessing the children in your charge, admonishing them, and praying for them. By the grace and strength that is in Christ Jesus, fathers can also make a difference in building up Timothys as other future leaders of the church.

The example of Paul with Timothy is worthy of our imitation to the extent that Paul is a "father *in Christ*," (1 Corinthians 4:15), following the "example of Christ" (11:1). Jesus Christ is the prototype of spiritual mentoring and fathering relationships. He mentored the twelve disciples like a close-knit family.

Our Next "Dad of the Week"

We conclude our study of fathers who made a difference by looking at Jesus. His understanding of fathering contrasts with misconceptions common to the first and twentieth centuries. In preparation for this final chapter, read John 8:12-59. This will bring us full circle, reconsidering what it means to be children of Abraham.

As you read Chapter 13 and review the previous twelve, you will reflect on what it means to be "Children of True Fathers." In reflecting on the dozen or so biblical forefathers we studied, I invite you to choose one father to follow as your inspirational example and run with it. (Make him your "Dad of the Year.") In Jesus' confrontation with Jewish leaders, this choice comes down to "Abraham, the Devil or God."

Endnotes

1. David DeWitt, *The Mature Man* (Vision House Publishing, Gresham, Oregon, 1994), page 155; also Stu Weber, *Tender Warrior* (Multnomah, Portland, Oregon: 1993), pages 57-58.

2. DeWitt, *The Mature Man*, page 155; also Weber, *Tender Warrior*, page 132.

3. Paul's preaching laid the foundation for the church at Corinth; hence, Paul was the "father" of the Corinthian believers (see 1 Corinthians 3:6,10; 4:15,17; 1 Timothy 1:2,18; also 2 Timothy 1:2; 2:1).

4. Excerpted from *Seven Promises of a Promise Keeper*, edited and published by Focus on the Family, Colorado Springs (copyright 1994, Promise Keepers 1994), where I tell my story in Glenn Wagner's chapter on mentoring relationships. All rights reserved and international copyright secured. Used with permission.

5. My understanding of teachable moments, mentoring relationships, and adult education in the church has been significantly shaped over the last two decades by Martha Leypoldt's book, *Learning Is Change* (Judson Press, Valley Forge, Pennsylvania: 1971).

6. An excellent resource for this is Linda and Richard Eyre, *Teaching Your Children Values* (A Fireside book, Division of Simon & Schuster, NYC: 1993). While not specifically Christian, the storehouse of practical wisdom and mentoring techniques in this book are consistent with the best of Christian education and the home school movement.

7. DeWitt, *The Mature Man*, pages 158-164. DeWitt goes so far as to say, "The most bumbling, inarticulate, tongue-tied, shy, introverted father is skyscrapers above the most educated, experienced, polished, cool youth director when it comes to teaching his kids about God. There is simply no one in the world who can have the influence of a natural father. Absolutely, positively, no one! Not any friend. Not any professional. Not any guardian. Not any step-parent. Not any foster parent. Not even any mother."

8. See 1 Corinthians 4:16; 11:1; also Galatians 4:12; Philippians 3:17; 1 Thessalonians 1:6; 2:14; 2 Thessalonians 3:7,9).

—•••—

"If you want to guarantee success,
choose with great care your grandfather."
Ben Franklin (1706-1790)

—•••—

"There are too many grandchildren of Christ in the world, those whose parents were Christians, but they aren't. Nowhere in the Bible does God claim grandchildren—just children born again by faith in Christ."
Bob Pierce (1914-1976)

—•••—

CHAPTER THIRTEEN

Children of True Fathers: Choosing a Father to Follow—"Abraham, the Devil or God"

The eighth chapter of John's Gospel, with its theme of Abraham and Jesus' relationship to God, is replete with implications for fathering. But I must open this heavy wrap-up discussion with a caveat: *I mean no ill will to my Jewish readers and sympathizers.* You will likely find offense in the decidedly hostile words in John's Gospel, like those in 8:44. That's because the Gospel of John probably was written against a background of Jewish-Christian hostility late in the first century.

I have no interest in stirring up ancient ethnic or religious hostilities, nor in advancing any classic arguments for Jesus' divinity or Messiahship. My reason for choosing this passage has nothing to do with John's original audience or harsh polemics, nor his purpose in helping Christians to bear witness to their Jewish brethren.

My purpose in drawing insights from John 8 is three-fold. First, I want us to empathize with classic misunderstandings of fatherhood common to Christians, pagans, and Jews. I also want to grasp Jesus' understanding of fatherhood in its biological, political, and spiritual dimensions. Jesus' discourse in John 8 suits my purpose, thirdly, to review the several father-types in Scripture, beginning with the Abraham typology, which holds together Jesus' discourse on fatherhood.

Classic misunderstandings of fatherhood

"The Jews" in John's Gospel represent those Jewish authorities hostile to Jesus, as not all rejected him, but many did believe he was the Messiah (8:30-31). Pharisees and other Jewish authorities seemed to question every statement of Jesus, particularly his references to being God's unique Son (8:14,18-19,23,42), the world's true Messiah (8:24-26,32,36), even Abraham's superior and predecessor (8:52-58).

To counter Jesus' exclusive and scandalous claims, "the Jews" claimed to be free of bondage by virtue of having Abraham as their father (8:33,39), insisting they were *not* "illegitimate children" but insinuating that (you know who) *was.*[1]

Presumptuous faith is not unique to ancient Israelites, but is also common to church-going believers. Jewish believers historically have presumed that being a child of Abraham meant having an inherited superiority, automatic privileges or guarantee of protective services. Many church-goers likewise presume, falsely, that their parental or political legacy entitles them to certain guarantees.

Jesus' understanding of fatherhood

Jesus contends, contrary to such presumptions, that a true descendent of Abraham or child of God is to be understood on a spiritual plane, not a biological or political one (8:31-41). And on the spiritual plane, Jesus raises the specter that the real "father" of "the Jews" (those hostile to Jesus) is not God but the devil (8:41-47).

Jesus seems to be saying, in effect, *God has no grandchildren; either you know Him firsthand as Father, or you don't know Him at all.*

The several father-types in Scripture

This same point is underscored by the experiences of other fathers in Scripture. Jacob could not prosper on the coattails of Isaac's relationship with the Father, but had to receive The Blessing directly from God. Likewise, Joseph could not fulfill his calling as a patriarch without leaving Jacob. He had to depend on God alone for deliverance, wisdom, prosperity, and forgiveness.

The daughters of Jephthah and Jairus may have known the Lord before adversity struck, at least through their fathers. But with death hanging over their heads, each made faith their own. Jairus's daughter, at least, had the privilege and joy of seeing the Lord Jesus, who called to her by name, back from the dead. No doubt father and daughter were never the same again after this healing encounter with the Great Physician.

Samson also had to learn the hard way that "God has no grandchildren." While leaning on the "rule" (Nazirite's vow) that his father Manoah had made and kept for him, Samson did okay. But because he did not know God's abiding presence for himself, Samson broke his vow and drifted from the Lord.

Eli's sons and Samuel also bear out the truth of this principle. The lives of Hophni and Phinehas were cut short because of their contempt for God's ways; yet as a foster father- priest, Eli succeeded with Samuel. He grew up dedicated to God's service and trained to hear and heed God's word for himself.

David was a "man after God's own heart," but his children were generally not. Solomon rode into power as David and Bathsheba pulled strings for him. However, Solomon soon had to ask for wisdom directly from God as the challenges of kingship became apparent.

Elisha could not rest on the laurels of his distinguished "father," either. God led him down his own lonely road into a charismatic and prophetic ministry as Elijah's successor.

Esther relied on Mordecai's faith and wise fathering to become the Queen of Persia. However, when crisis management and divine intervention were needed, she was ready. Esther depended on God through days of prayer and fasting, trusting that God's will would be done through her.

Joseph also had this quality of faith on behalf of his adopted child, Jesus. In response to angelic visitors and divine intervention, Joseph believed in Jesus, had him dedicated in the temple *before* Jesus would become the "reason for the season." As Joseph's son, Jesus' received a father's blessing from him, and as God's Son, received the blessing of directly knowing God. ("You are my Son whom I love; with You I am well pleased.")

Timothy was reared by a "father in Christ" to be a child of God in his own right and then a father in the faith to still others.

This brings us full circle to Abraham, the "father of many nations" (Genesis 17:5) and "the father of all who believe" (Romans 4:11). So it is not just "the Jews" who can claim that "Abraham is our father" (John 8:39).

While children cannot choose their biological fathers, much less their grandfathers, these biblical examples seem to suggest that we do choose our spiritual fathers. We choose a father to follow by deciding what to believe, the way to behave, and the mentor to imitate. Jesus says as much when he points out, "If you were Abraham's children, . . .then you would do the things Abraham did" (John 8:39).

Thus, by doing the things these biblical forefathers did, we are choosing fathers who will make a difference in our lives. In turn, we choose to become fathers who make a difference in still other lives.

QUESTIONS FOR GROUP WARM-UP

These get-acquainted questions can be answered without reading the thematic introduction or doing the Bible study for this chapter.

1. We have all imagined what it might be like to be reared in another household by another set of parents. If the choice were yours to turn back the clock, who would you want for your father? Why? Choose from a TV family (Column 1), a biblical family (Column 2), and a real-life acquaintance.[2]

Column 1
- ☐ The Cleavers (*Leave It to Beaver*)
- ☐ The Waltons
- ☐ The Bunkers (*All in the Family*)
- ☐ The Seavers (*Growing Pains*)
- ☐ The Huxtables (*The Cosby Show*)
- ☐ The Keatons (*Family Ties*)
- ☐ The Conners (*Roseanne*)

Column 2
- ☐ Abraham
- ☐ Jacob
- ☐ Jephthah or Jairus
- ☐ Manoah
- ☐ Eli
- ☐ David
- ☐ Solomon

- ☐ The Andersons (*Father Knows Best*)
- ☐ The Nelsons (*Ozzie and Harriet*)
- ☐ The Bundys (*Married with Children*)
- ☐ The Ricardos (*I Love Lucy*)
- ☐ The Addams Family
- ☐ The Simpsons
- ☐ The Brady Bunch
- ☐ The Cartwrights (*Bonanza*)
- ☐ Elijah
- ☐ Mordecai
- ☐ Joseph
- ☐ The Prodigal's Father
- ☐ Paul or Barnabas
- ☐ Other (please name):

2. Have your children ever wished you would "drop dead" or "get lost?" Perhaps they may have wanted to run away, cut you off, or stop visiting you. How did you feel then? What did you do in response? (If your children are not old enough to state such fanciful wishes or strong feelings, empathize with your father or with older fathers in your group who will have experienced this.)

Questions for Bible Study

Read John 8:12-59. Then continue your group study by individually answering these questions and sharing with others from your notes.

3. What did Jesus mean by saying, "I know where I came from and where I am going [but you do not]" (John 8:14)?

- ☐ Jesus knew God first-hand, but the Pharisees did not (8:19).
- ☐ Jesus was alleged to have no earthly or legitimate father (8:19,23).
- ☐ Jesus was going to die without sin and go to heaven, but the Pharisees would die in their sins and go to hell (8:21-24).
- ☐ Jesus was sent to earth with a unique mission, to die for our sin and return to heaven victorious over death. He could then judge the living and the dead and intercede for us (8:24-28).
- ☐ Jesus was secure in his heavenly Father's presence and love. Their relationship surpasses what any of us will ever have with our earthly fathers (8:29).
- ☐ Jesus was obedient to his Father in heaven, pleasing Him always (8:29).
- ☐ Other (please explain):

4. With what false assumptions about fatherhood, slavery, sonship, discipleship, and truth are the Pharisees operating?

5. Why do you suppose Jesus' language remained unclear to the original hearers (8:19,21,23,25,27,41-47,51,57)?

When and how will their spiritual darkness be lifted (8:17-20,23-24,28,31-32,36,51)?

6. What distinguished who "belongs to God" and who does not?

Likewise, who can claim Abraham as their father and who can not?

7. Review all the *if*-clauses in John 8:12-59. What will happen in each case...

a. If Jesus testifies alone on His own behalf (8:14)?

b. If Jesus stood in judgment (8:16)?

c. If you really knew Jesus (8:19)?

d. If you do not believe that Jesus is the Messiah (8:24)?

e. If you hold to Jesus' teaching (8:31)?

f. If the Son sets you free (8:36)?

g. If you were Abraham's children (8:39)?

h. If God were your Father (8:42)?

i. If Jesus is telling the truth (8:46)?

j. If anyone keeps Jesus' word (8:51)?

k. If Jesus were to selfishly seek glory (8:54)?

l. If Jesus said He did not know God (8:55)?

Questions for Application

This third set of questions is designed to bring the point home to yourself and other fathers.

8. Which of the above conditions (**a** to **l**) apply to *you*? (Which were once true of you? Which are true of you now? Which do you want to be true of you by the time you die?)

9. How can you make room for God's word in your life (8:37,51) as a child of God, disciple of Christ, and father in the faith?

- ☐ The example of fathers in this group taking Scripture seriously has inspired me to do likewise.
- ☐ I will review the fathers in this book and "the rest of the story" in each case.
- ☐ I will join/start a men's group that does Bible study each week.
- ☐ I will commit myself to a read-through-the-Bible plan next year.
- ☐ I will commit myself to read the Bible tomorrow.
- ☐ I will apply what I have learned from *Fathers Who Made a Difference* before I try to pack any more Bible knowledge into my brain.
- ☐ I will choose one biblical forefather to follow as my mentor and learn from all that he did right and all that he did wrong.
- ☐ Other (please explain):

10. Which one biblical forefather would you choose to follow as your "Dad of the Year" mentor and why? (How is your situation parallel to the biblical one? What life lessons have your name on them? The Table of Contents may serve as a helpful checklist.)

The Rest of the Story

We at Broadman & Holman and the National Center for Fathering want to hear from you. We want to help you identify your fathering strengths, assess your fathering pattern and equip other fathers. For this purpose, we have inserted in this book the "Discovering Your Fathering Pattern" designed by the National Center for Fathering. To receive more feedback on your fathering pattern, and to receive the *Today's Dads* magazine, you simply complete the enclosed 5-step survey and mail it in.

If you need more copies of this survey for a group or class you are leading, please write National Center for Fathering, 10200 W. 75th Street, Suite 267, Shawnee, Kansas 66204, or call 1-800/593-DADS.

Behind every able man. . .there are always other able men. That man-centered saying is a welcome twist on the more familiar "female-power-behind-the-throne" proverb. I actually found this proverb in a Chinese fortune cookie I broke into as I was in the final stages of writing this book. Sounds promising and fortunate, indeed!

As this study ends, there are reasons for thanksgiving.

For the last thirteen weeks or so, the men in your group have stood together. You also have the host of children and young Elishas and Timothys whom you will "father," in every sense of that pregnant and nurturing word. You may also be thanking God for the particular Barnabas who has seen the grace of God at work in you. If you have a Jacob who strives and passes along his blessing to you, or an Abraham who will pray for and persevere with you, you have all the more reason to give thanks.

If you are wounded or fatherless, you may thank God for the David or Mordecai in your life who will keep a covenant promise to stand by you and yours through thick and thin. If you are a card-carrying Promise Keeper, give thanks for promise keepers like Eli and Manoah who may have taken special vows to raise and mentor you right.

Having thanked all those who have stood behind me to make this project possible at the front end, I now join this "cloud of many witnesses" who stand behind all of us. With Christ, we stand ready to complete the good work of fathering which he began and continues in each of us.

Endnotes

1. This inference from John 8:41 ("*We* are not illegitimate [but you are]") was made explicit by early Church Fathers (e.g., Origen), who alleged that the Jews charged Jesus was born of fornication. See Chapter 10 for more discussion about the very real doubts and scandal surrounding Jesus' birth parents. In keeping with orthodox Christian tradition, we can safely assert that Jesus was born of Mary *to* Joseph, and that Jesus was not *of* Joseph, nor *by* the agency of Joseph, but was conceived by the Holy Spirit (Matthew 3:17; Luke 1:32-35; Hebrews 1:5).

2. The selections of TV families (Column 1) are taken from William Cutler and Richard Peace, *Blended Families* (Serendipity House, Littleton, CO: 1990), page 17. Used with permission.